LIVING LENT

(Revised Edition)

MARIANNE DORMAN

Living Lent

Published by Wheatmark™
610 East Delano Street, Suite 104, Tucson, Arizona 85705 U.S.A.
www.wheatmark.com

International Standard Book Number: 9781587369278
Library of Congress Control Number: 2007933246

TO THE GLORY OF GOD
AND
IN THANKSGIVING
FOR THOSE
WHO WITNESS
TO
THE CATHOLIC FAITH
AND
IN MEMORY
OF
JOHN HOPE
AND
AUSTIN DAY

Welcome dear feast of Lent: who loves not thee,
He loves not Temperance, or Authority.
But is composed of passion.
The Scripture bids us fast; the church says, Now:
Give to thy mother what thou wouldst allow
To every Corporation. ...

True Christians should be glad of an occasion
To use their temperance, seeking no evasion,
When good is seasonable;
Unless Authority, which should increase
The obligation in us, make it less,
And Power itself disable. ...

'Tis true, we cannot reach Christ's fortieth day;
Yet to go part of that religious way
Is better than to rest:
We cannot reach our Saviour's purity;
Yet are we bid, Be holy e'en as He.
In both let's do our best.

Who goes in the way which Christ has gone,
Is much more sure to meet with Him, than one
That travelleth by-ways.
Perhaps my God, though he be far before,
May turn, and take me by the hand, and more,
May strengthen my decays.

Yet, Lord, instruct us to improve our fast
By starving sin, and taking such repast
As may our faults control:
That ev'ry man may revel at his door,
Not in his parlour; banqueting the poor,
And among those his soul.

M. Dorman, *The Life of Glory* (Durham, 1992), pp. 35-7.

FOREWORD

MARIANNE DORMAN'S MEDITATIONS FOR Lent have grown out of her own disciplined reflections on the Christian gospel and tradition; they have already been prayed through, and this gives them a special depth and resonance. She writes as someone whose own Christian faith is informed by a wide range of reading and scholarship, especially in the golden age of Anglican prose, the early seventeenth century; and her own writing is, in the best sense, 'classical' in its style and concerns. She does not strive after quick emotional effects or seek up a flow of bright ideas, but composes her reflections in the expectation that they will be read as they have been written, with seriousness, slowly and attentively. They will anchor the reader in a sober appreciation of the abiding themes of Christian belief, and will stimulate to prayer. I am grateful for her writing, and am happy to commend it to others looking for devotional writing that is traditional without being defensive and committed without being sentimental or mindless. She stands in a worthy succession.

Rowan Williams
Bishop of Monmouth.
(Archbishop of Canterbury
when I revised this book in 2007).

PREFACE

THIS IS A REVISED edition of *Living Lent* first published in 1992. In making this revision I have included the daily readings for Lent and the Sundays that were lacking in the original edition. As Catholic Christians become more aware of the importance of Scripture in their lives, I want to encourage them to read the sacred pages and discover how relevant they are for our daily living.

Thus this book is designed for living out our Catholic Faith. It is essential to understand there should be no separation between the holy and the human as divinity and humanity are one through Christ. Hence for each day of Lent an aspect of our Christian faith is presented.

The meditation for each day ends with a short prayer. I encourage you to use this as a guide for making your own. Spontaneous prayer is a way of growing in the life of the Holy Spirit. At first you may feel clumsy but it becomes easier with practice.

Lent ends on Holy Thursday morning to give way to the Triduum. This is the most important time of the Christian Year when the Church celebrates one continuous Liturgy but in three acts - the passion, death and resurrection of Christ.

In writing this revised edition I am still conscious of what I owe to so many for teaching me through word and example the Christian faith and how it must be lived out. Shortly after becoming a practising Christian in my mid-teens I began attending Christ Church St. Laurence in Sydney, Australia. How fortunate I was to be taught the Catholic Faith by Father John Hope, the rector. He certainly planted the seeds, which have been watered by many ever since, including his successor, Fr. Austin Day.

The first edition of this book was written shortly after coming to Oxford in the late 1980's. Here too I was blessed by the ministry of various priests. Three come to mind readily: Dr. Rowan Williams who was then Lady Margaret Professor and Canon of Christ Church, Oxford and now Archbishop of Canterbury. He encouraged me to write amongst other things. Canon Donald Allchin who was then Director of the St. Theosevia Centre, Oxford, and now Professor Emeritus of Church History at Bangor; and Dr. Jeffrey John who was then Dean of Divinity at Magdalen College, Oxford, and now Dean at St. Alban's Abbey.

I am also grateful to the past President of Magdalen College, Oxford, Mr. A. Smith, and Dr. J. Gregg of the Physics Department who made it possible for me to use as the cover a reproduction of Christ Bearing the Cross, attributed to the seventeenth-century Spanish painter Valdes Leal. Since 1745 this painting has hung above the altar in the chapel. It was given to the College by William Freeman of Hamels in Hertfordshire, a former gentleman commoner of this College.

Previously this painting had a rather adventurous history. It was amongst the treasures looted by James Butler, Duke of Ormonde in 1702 when the English fleet under Admiral Sir George Rooke entered the harbour of Vigo, Spain on 12th October 1702 and seized the Spanish treasure galleons. Sometime afterwards it came into the possession of Walter Freeman.

I am particularly grateful to use this painting for the cover, not only because it was a source of meditation for me over the years I attended Mass in Magdalen College, but also because the carrying of the cross is the core of the Christian life. I trust Leal's painting will in itself be a source of deep reflection during Lent.

The basic text for quotations from the Bible is the Authorized Version while the Psalms are from the Prayer Book with slight changes to modernize archaic words.

Have a wonderful Lent, Triduum and a joyful Easter.

Greenbank, WA. U.S.A.
Corpus Christi, 2007.

ABBREVIATIONS AND BIBLIOGRAPHY

Anselm   *The Prayers and Meditations of St. Anselm with The Prosalgion* (Harmondsworth, 1973).

Andrewes   *The Works of Lancelot Andrewes*, 11 vols (Oxford, 1841 - 1854).

Augustine   *The Confessions of St. Augustine*, Vol.1 (The Library of The Fathers, London, 1838).

Bernard   *Cantica Canticorum*, Eighty-six Sermons on the Song of Solomon, trans. and ed. by S. J. Eales (London, 1895).

Bloom   "The Metropolitan Anthony Bloom of Sourzh; A Russian Orthodox Bishop in London", *Sobornost Review* 12 (1979).

C.P.D.   *The Catholic Prayer Book,* compiled by Mons. M. Buckley (London, 1999).

Cloud   *The Cloud of Unknowing*, ed. Fr. A. Baker, O.S.B (London, 1871).

Clement   *Early Christian Writers, The Apostolic Fathers* (Harmondsworth, 1968).

Cosin   *The Works of The Rt. Rev'd Father in God, John Cosin, Lord Bishop of Durham,* 5 vols (Oxford, 1843 - 55).

Donne, *A Sermon*   *A Sermon Preached to The King's Majesty at Whitehall, 24th February, 1625/26 by John Donne, Dean of St. Paul's* (London, 1626).

Donne, *Eighty Sermons* *Eighty Sermons preached by ... John Donne, D.D* (London, 1640).

Donne, *Fifty Sermons*   *Fifty Sermons preached by ... John Donne, D.D* (London, 1649).

Donne, *Twenty-six Sermons*	*Twenty-six Sermons preached by ... John Donne, D.D* (London, 1662).
Dorman	M. Dorman, *The Life of Glory* (Durham, 1992).
New English Hymnal	*The New English Hymnal*, Melody Edition (Norwich, 1986).
Evelyn	*A Devotionary Book of John Evelyn of Wotton, 1620 – 1706*, ed. W. Frere (London, 1936).
Farindon	*The Sermons of the Rev. Anthony Farindon, B.D., with his life*, 4 vols (London, 1849).
Frank	*Sermons by Mark Frank, D.D.* 2 vols (Oxford, 1849).
Fulman	*The works of the Reverend and Learned Henry Hammond, D.D.*, ed. W.Fulman, 4 vols (London, 1874).
Gore	J. Gore, *The Way to Prosper* (London, 1646).
Gore, *Oracle*	J. Gore, *The Oracle* (London, 1646).
Hammond	*Thirty-One Sermons Preached on Several Occasions by Henry Hammond*, 2 vols (Oxford, 1849).
Heber	*The Whole Works of The Right Reverend Jeremy Taylor, D.D.* ed. R. Heber, 15 vols (London, 1822).
Hilton	W. Hilton, *The Scale of Perfection* (London, 1901).
Hopkins, *God's Grandeur*	*The Poems of Gerard Manley Hopkins*, ed. Robert Bridges (London, 1918).
Hopkins, *Pied Beauty*	*The Poems of Gerard Manley Hopkins*, ed. Robert Bridges (London, 1918).
Hooker	*The Works of Richard Hooker*, ed. J. Keble, 3 vols (Oxford, 1874).
John of the Cross	*The Complete Works of St. John of the Cross*, trans and ed. By D. Lewis, 2 vols (London, 1867).
Julian of Norwich	Julian of Norwich, *Revelations of Divine Love* (London, 1877).

Kronstadt, *Counsels* *The Spiritual Counsels of Father John of Kronstadt*, ed. W. J. Grisbrooke (London, 1966).

Kronstadt, *Life* Bishop Alexander (Semenoff-Tian- Chansky) *Father John of Kronstadt: A Life* (London, 1979).

Milner-White *My God, My Glory* (London, 1961).

Nicodemus *The Gospel of Nicodemus*, trans. by A. Westcott (London, 1915).

Orthodox Manual F. W. Campbell, *A Little Orthodox Manual* (London, 1911).

Rolle *Selected Works of Richard Rolle*, ed. G. C. Heseltine (London, 1930).

Sanderson *Sermons by the Rt. Rev'd Fr. In God, Robert Sanderson, Late Lord Bishop of Lincoln, with a life of the Author by Isaac Walton*, 2 vols (London, 1841).

Shakespeare W. Shakespeare, *The Most Excellent History of The Merchant of Venice* (London, 1600).

Shelford R. Shelford, *Five Pious and Learned Discourses* (Cambridge,1635).

Singh Sadhu Sundar Singh, *At the Master's Feet*, trans. by the Rev'd. A. and Mrs Parker (London, 1922).

Sparrow A. Sparrow, *The Confession of Sins and The Power of Absolution* (London, 1637).

Spenser *Easter Morning*, in *A Treasury of Christian Verse* (London, 1959).

St. Francis *Praying with St. Francis*, eds. R. J. Armstrong and I. C. Brady (London, 1989).

Sydenham H. Sydenham, *The Rich Man's Warning Peece* (London, 1630).

Taylor *The Whole Works of the Rt. Revd. Jeremy Taylor*, ed. C. P. Eden, 10 vols (London, 1844 - 57).

The Prayer of Jesus	A Monk of the Eastern Church, (Lev Gillet), *The Prayer of Jesus*, trans. by a monk of the Western Church (New York, 1967).

CONTENTS

INTRODUCTION

WELCOME FEAST OF LENT. Like Herbert and so many countless Christians down the centuries, I always thank God that the Church was wise enough to set aside forty days before the great feast of Easter as a special time for renewing and recharging one's spiritual life through exercising the disciplines of fasting, self-denial, repentance, amendment of life, prayer, meditation and contemplation.

Ideally the way we live Lent should be the way we live the whole year, but one way and another we lapse here and there - not being so constant in our prayer time, forgetting about acts of self-denials, not keeping the other fast and abstinence days of the Christian year, neglecting the needs of our brothers and sisters, losing the vision of our true humanity, and so on. Hopefully by keeping a good Lent this year it will encourage us to continue living in such a manner all year.

Lent is a time for stillness and to breathe in God. By being alone with Him, we allow Him to take over and direct our lives.

Lent is a time for service, when we spend less time on ourselves in order to help others.

Lent is a time to consider that God has given each one of us gifts which are unique. These we must recognize as well as being receptive to the gifts of others. It is thus a time for sharing our talents and being enriched.

Lent is a time for an awareness of the presence and activity of the Holy Spirit within us and all creation, nothing remains static. As we are part of this creation we have to recognize that we must keep on growing, but to do this we must be satiated with the Holy Spirit. One sign of growth is to recognize our sinfulness that stunts growth. This season is thus that special time when penitence and creativity can fuse.

Lent is a time to be prayerful people. Perhaps at the moment some of us regard prayer as a bit like a shop window. It is very attractive to look at, but we never venture inside to buy. If we have never taken prayer seriously this is the time to start. Prayer is the means by which we transform our lives by adding that divine dimension to it. As John of Kronstadt reminds us, praying should be as easy as thinking.[1]

Lent is a time to discover who I am. In other words do I see myself as God sees me? Am I becoming the person He wants me to be? Or am I living behind some mask? Are there some things in my life to which I have closed my eyes? Are there aspects of my life I should work on?

Every Lent I cannot help but ponder on Lancelot Andrewes' warning that this might be our last Lent, our last time to repent or turn to God. He compared the necessity of our repentance at the beginning of Lent with the example of those birds described in Jeremiah (8.7) that know instinctively the time to return and do it. "'The stork in the air knows her appointed times, and the turtle, the crane and the swallow observe the time of their coming; but my people know not the judgment of the Lord.'" He therefore urges us to react just as instinctively as these birds do for their "appointed times" for returning. That "appointed time" for them is "now" and it is for us too. "Who knows whether he will live to see them return anymore?…It may be the last Spring, the last swallow-time, the last Wednesday of this name or nature, we shall ever live." Hence we should not "'let this time slip' by without responding to it."[2]

Lent of course gives way to the Triduum, the three most important days in the Christian year when we celebrate our redemption and restoration by our Lord Jesus Christ. We journey to Jerusalem with our Saviour so that we too can enter into His passion, death and then His resurrection. Death no longer has its sting. Christ has triumphed over it and sin and all evil. How blessed we are in having a Saviour!

---

1   Kronstradt, *Counsels*, pp. 27-8.
2   Andrewes, Vol. 1, pp. 338, 350-1, 353.

PREPARATION

Prepare to meet your God.
Amos 4.12.

Make me a clean heart O God and
renew a right spirit within me.
Psalm 51.10.

WITH ANY IMPORTANT OCCASION in life such as marriage, an examination or the visit of a dear friend we make preparation, often a great lengths. We do not wait until the day has arrived before we start because that is like acting as the foolish virgins did in the Gospel.

Lent, as it is an important event in the life of Christians each year, needs similar planning. In order to keep this season with any kind of discipline and devotion we must be ready. So we have this day, especially set aside to examine our consciences, and to be shriven of our sins (hence the name Shrove Tuesday). Assured of God forgiveness in the sacrament of Penance/Reconciliation we have the grace to undertake our Lenten journey. That journey often involves making resolutions, but these should not be seen just as an exercise of will power, but rather a way to help us grow in love, not only for God but also for our neighbour. As St. Basil once pointed out it is no use to abstain from meat, if we devour our brother. To love unconditionally all those with whom we come in contact is one of the most difficult tasks to accomplish and we cannot do it without God's grace. Therefore it is imperative to spend time, and plenty of it, simply with God and allow ourselves to absorb His generous gifts. Then grace will prevail

3

and the fruits of the Spirit will begin to flourish in our lives as we endeavour to gain mastery over our sins.

Perhaps you wonder what resolutions you should make. My suggestion about making resolutions is that they are only effective if they allow us the opportunity to grow in our relationship with Christ and add quality to our lives. In making resolutions we must never lose sight that Lent is essentially our preparation for the Triduum, those three days that celebrate the institution of the Eucharist, the passion and death of Christ, His descent into hell and His glorious resurrection (Holy Thursday to the Easter Vigil). Thus all that we do during Lent should lead us to Jerusalem with Christ as He endures his Passion, Death and Resurrection. As Clement, a presbyter in the Church of Rome at the end of the first century expressed it, "Let us fix our thoughts on the blood of Christ and reflect how precious it is in the eyes of God, since it was poured out for our salvation and has brought the grace of repentance to all the world."[3]

The Triduum finishes with the Resurrection message that should fix out thoughts on heaven, our eventual home. Mark Frank in one of his Lenten sermons tells us that "this holy time of Lent is indeed a time for 'mastery' with our corruptions, ... a time of holy exercises upon the 'corruptible' earth to obtain a crown 'incorruptible' in the heavens."[4] In this very secular world this is good advice for us to contemplate during Lent as our citizenship is in heaven. Thus Lent is the perfect time to change, let go or to improve in order to win that incorruptible crown as St. Paul tells us in his letter to the Corinthians (1 Cor. 15.53-4).

Let us make sure then that our preparation is such that we have a solid foundation to make our lives after Lent purposeful, prayerful and profound.

Heavenly Father we thank You for all Your blessings that You shower upon Your children. Help me to make this Lent a growing time but also a reflective time to see myself as You see me in my preparation for the passion, death and resurrection of Your Son. Amen.

---

3   Clement, p.26.
4   Frank, Vol. 2, p. 1.

FASTING

*Turn you even to me, says the Lord, with
all your heart, and with fasting, and with
weeping, and with mourning.*

Joel 2. 12.

Full Readings: Joel 2.12-18; Psalm 51.3-6, 12-14, 17; 2 Corinthians 5.20 -
6.2; Matthew 6.1-6, 16-18.

THIS MOST SOLEMN DAY ushers in forty days of mortification, fasting
and preparation (the Sundays during Lent are excluded) for the Triduum. If we keep Ash Wednesday as it is meant to be observed as a
day of fasting and prayer, as evident from the selected readings for
this day, it will help us immensely to keep a good Lent. How we fast
depends on the individual and of course age. Some are able to fast
all day and eat one light meal in the evening; others because of the
nature of his/her work, or medical problem(s) need to have breakfast.
However we all should be able to eat more frugally by having a small
breakfast and a light supper. For Catholics a fast day means eating
one whole meal and the other two must not be more than one whole
meal, and without snacking in between.

Undoubtedly most of us eat and drink too much. Rather than eating when our bodies need food, and drinking when we are thirsty, we
usually eat or drink for some kind of pleasure. Lent is a superb time
to subdue our eating and drinking indulgences and learn to monitor
our body respectfully and healthfully. It is after all the temple of the
living Spirit. Fasting should also teach us not to be wasteful and to

5

become more conscious of the plight of millions of our brothers and sisters around the world who are dying from hunger and who would gladly eat the crusts we cut off our bread and discard.

Fasting also helps us to mortify the flesh. "We must deny our own wills, our appetites of gluttony and drunkenness, ... for the purchase of temperance," preached the Caroline Divine, Jeremy Taylor. He also reminded us it is a means whereby "the will of man may humbly obey God, and absolutely rule its inferior faculties," and therefore mortification is essential if we want to grow spiritually, for without it, "we neither can love to pray, nor can God love to hear us."[5]

However as suggested fasting is not simply a matter of exercising self discipline and showing how strong willed we can be. Although discipline there must be, it is done as an act of love for Christ in thanksgiving for the many blessings He has given us through His passion and to help us to grow in holiness. "Fasting is one of the nails of the cross to which the flesh is fastened, that it rise not, [and] lust not 'against the spirit,'" suggested Andrewes.[6] When it is accompanied with prayer it is a powerful spiritual exercise.

Fasting also enables us to imitate Christ. Not only do we have His commendation for it by His forty days in the wilderness, but we also have those other times when He withdrew from the crowds to lonely places to fast and pray to His Father. We also have His specific teaching on it as we heard in today's Gospel. As Frank preached:

We have (1) our Master's example for our fasting; even for the fast we are in, …We have (2) his precept and prediction for fasting too, when he should be gone; we have (3) his order and direction how to do it – 'When you fast,' do thus and thus. We have (4) S. Paul telling us of a giving ourselves to it, making a business of it. We have (5) all the ages of our Christianity severely using it. We have (6) here an excellent end of it, the keeping under of the body: and indeed that I need not prove; it is the fault we find with it 'that it weakens the knees and dries up the flesh,' - that it agrees not with our bodies. No more it should: that is the virtue of it. And it being of that virtue, and we having so good example, so plain precept, so sober direction, so strict

5   Taylor, Vol. 2, pp. 172 - 3.
6   Andrewes, Vol. 1, p. 380.

practice, so long custom, to commend us to it, I know not where it sticks that it is performed no better.[7]

These days, it has become fashionable to fast in order to be slim and healthy, but it has always been fashionable in the Church to deny the body food and drink in order to have a healthy soul. Let this be fashionable for us this Lent as we prepare for the greatest festival of the Christian year.

Heavenly Father, Your dear Son showed us the importance of fasting. Let me gladly endure some bodily discomforts this Lent through fasting and mortification for the sake of the kingdom. Amen.

---

7   Frank, Vol. 1, p. 407.

SELF DENIAL

'If man will come after me, let him deny himself,
and take up his cross daily, and follow me.'

Luke 9. 23.

Full Readings: Deuteronomy 30.15-20; Psalm 1. 1-6; Luke 9.22-25.

CLOSELY AKIN TO FASTING is abstinence or self-denial as these too mortify the flesh. As well as fasting on the set fast days of Lent, we are also bidden to abstain. Perhaps this is what some refer to as 'giving up' for Lent, but it involves more than not having sugar in coffee or a sherry before dinner. Of course it should mean forgoing something we like very much, but surely it should also teach us as Christians that we live more frugally than most of us do. Looked at positively, abstinence is a form of self-denial when we impose that act of discipline on ourselves in order to turn it into a means of prayer and devotion, and of becoming more Christ-like.

Frank insisted that "if we keep not our bodies low, they will keep us low; if we bring not them into subjection, they will bring us into slavery; they will cast us away, if we cast away too much upon them." The only "way to cure our fears, to confirm our hopes, to help our weaknesses, to beat back temptations, to establish our titles and rights to heaven, to make God's grace effectual upon us, - to sanctify our prayers, and preachings, and all our labours, to the glory of a reward," is by mortifying or denying the flesh.[8]

This self denial is a powerful way to unite ourselves with our

---

8   Ibid., p. 414.

8

dear Lord in His temptation and passion. It is a means to live with Jesus constantly throughout the day, and is also a means of intercessory prayer for our brothers and sisters in our world. I usually listen to the six o'clock news each morning with the intention of keeping before me that day the needs of others and the problems of the world before Morning Prayer. During the day whenever I make an act of self denial, be it all so small, I try to unite it with an ejaculatory prayer for the someone(s) or something(s) in this world needing the power of prayer in Christ's name.

Apart from abstaining from some kind of food and drink for all of Lent, there are also daily self-denials of food and drink we can make. For instance, we can decide on a particular day we shall eat our bread without margarine or butter, or we shall forgo that second cup of coffee we love so much at breakfast, or to drink water rather than fruit juice or wine with our dinner.

Do not think however that acts of self-denial are limited to meal times. There are other ways too. Some of these include forgoing: the comfort of listening to the radio and music, watching television, reading a daily newspaper or novel, attending concerts or the theatre. Instead we spend the time in prayer and/or acts of charity. Like food or drink some of these can be denied for all of Lent or on a daily basis. Remember "abstinence is a virtue".[9]

Furthermore self-denial enables us to be more appreciative of how bountifully God has blessed us. That bounty we recognize truly on Easter day as we celebrate the joys of the Resurrection not only by attending the Paschal ceremonies but also over our Paschal dinner. Nothing tastes so good as when we have gone without it for forty days! It is true Paschal joy! So let us this Lent deny ourselves of some of the pleasures of our life as Christ did in order to make our souls more strong in His service and to value what we have been given.

Dear Lord, help me to make acts of self-denials for You during this Lent. May they also enable me to empathize with the suffering of many in this world who are starving, homeless, tortured, imprisoned unjustly or suffer any other kind of oppressions. Amen.

---

9   Andrewes, Vol. 1, p. 380.

FRIDAY AFTER ASH WEDNESDAY

ALMSGIVING

Is not this the fast that I have chosen? ...
Is it not to share your bread with the hungry,
and ...bring the poor...to your house?

Isaiah 58. 6- 7.

Full Readings: Isaiah 58.1-9; Psalm 51. 3-6, 18-19; Matthew 9.14-15.

ANOTHER PURPOSE FOR FASTING and abstinence is to give to others what we would normally have for ourselves. It is simply no good to practise those acts of self-discipline, as to-day's reading from Isaiah makes clear, unless we are prepared to share them with our brothers and sisters. One of the common ways of doing this during Lent has been donating the equivalent cost of what we have given up towards a missionary or charitable organization. Although this is commend-able, in some ways I think this sours our efforts because it is all so easy to put money in an envelope. To me the more Christian way would be to take food and spend a little time with someone who longs for both, especially the latter. Thus almsgiving means giving of ourselves and being a doing Christian.

Alas, all too often our doing in Lent is thought of in terms of at-tending a bible study group or something similar. Although there is nothing wrong with this, may I suggest that perhaps a more Christ-like use of that time would be to visit old Joe or Mary who live alone, or the young Vietnamese family struggling to cope with speaking English or to assist at the drop-out centre or the local hospital. There are so many souls desperate for companionship. We do not have to look very far from our front door to see that the world is begging for friendship, compassion and assistance. If we do not know of any, our parish priest certainly will or should. If not, in the community there are organizations responsible for giving relief to the needy which will gladly accept another helping hand. Lent offers this opportunity to start.

Indeed those who give "with a true intent to relieve the poor ... the distressed", end up giving themselves "more good". However those who "will part nothing to the poor" forfeit their goods to God and render themselves to His exacting judgment, preached Gore.[10] Furthermore a contemporary, Anthony Farindon, reminds us that the time may come when we are in a similar position to these people, and issued this warning: "For when you see a man you behold yourself as in a glass. In him you behold yourself, now cheerful, and [soon] drooping; now standing, and anon sinking; now in purple, and anon naked; now full and anon hungry."[11]

Another Caroline Divine, John Donne, insisted that our "holy works" and our "lives are appointed by God to preach to one another." Indeed our "good works" are necessary to make our faith alive and have meaning and purpose. Both faith and our works are based upon the two great commandments given by Christ in the Gospel "to love God, and love our neighbour." Therefore in this world faith and work go hand in hand and we stand upon both: "faith" revealed in our love for God, and "works in the sight of man." Moreover "our faith grows into a better state, and into a better liking, by our good works," so that "faith is perfected by working; for, *faith is dead*, without breath, without spirit, if it be *without works*." Hence "we are created, we are baptized, we are adopted for good works", and although "faith has a pre-eminence because works grow out of it, ... yet works have the pre-eminence" in the sense "that they include faith in them, and that they dilate, and diffuse, and spread themselves more declaratory, than faith does." More importantly "our good works are more ours, than our faith is," because faith we "have received", while our works is what "we have done". Though faith is "the only true root" for belief "in this life", on Judgment day, we shall be judged "by our

---

10 Gore, p. 43.
11 Farindon, Vol. 1, p. 237.

fruits", that is the produce of "good works" and not by faith.[12] Let us be generous this Lent in giving to others.

My dear Saviour who gave all, even Your life so that I may have eternal life, teach me that faith and fasting are nothing unless accompanied by my giving of self, talents, goods and time to others in Your name. Amen.

12 Donne, *Fifty Sermons*, pp. 65, 273 - 3; 458; Donne, *Eighty Sermons*, pp. 78 - 9, 82 - 3; Donne, *Twenty-six Sermons*, p. 286.

Follow Me

'Follow me.'

Luke 5. 28.

Full Readings: Isaiah 58.9-14; Psalm 86. 1-6; Luke 5.27 – 32.

THE GOSPEL READING TELLS of the calling of Levi, a tax collector for the Roman government, who immediately left his desk after hearing Christ's words "Follow me". He then entertained Jesus at a banquet. How can we imitate Levi's example and be a true follower of our Lord in all the perplexities that modern society offers?

If we are going to give God a chance to speak to us, and let His will be known to us, then we have to spend some time each day by simply stilling ourselves. That means excluding everything out of our mind and soul and in fact our whole being, except God Himself. We must "steal away from [our] earthly occasions ... to do the business of the heavenly Father," stated Gore.[13] The most productive way is to have time regularly in just being with God, preferably before the Blessed Sacrament and so give God a chance to speak to us and for us to hear. After all Mary would never have heard the angel's message if she had not learnt to still herself.

St. Anselm in the first chapter of *Proslogion* spoke of the importance of being alone and still.

> Come now, ... from your daily employment, escape for a moment from the tumults of your thoughts. Put aside your weighty

---

13 Gore, *Oracle*, p. 15.

cares, let your burdensome distractions wait, free yourself awhile for God and rest awhile in Him.

Enter the inner chamber of your soul, shut out everything except God and that which can help you in seeking Him, and when you have shut the door, seek him.[14]

As intimated Gore too recommend aloneness. "There is no such time for a man to converse with God, and ... to acquaint himself with the Lord, as when he is solitary, private and alone." Then if anything is grieving "a man, or lie heavy upon his conscience, ... he may freely disburden his heart into the bosom of God."[15] This last point is important because we cannot be still if our soul is burdened with worries.

For those who have never practised stillness and waiting upon God, it may seem a too difficult task to attempt. Let me assure you it is not too difficult for anyone, and once begun, daily life without it will seem empty. There will always be a gnawing, almost a hunger. I know that if for some reason I have missed out on my quiet time, through travelling or for some other reason, there always seem to be something wrong all day, as if I am like my watch which has stopped because I have not wound it. The divine within tells me that "My soul truly [must wait] still upon God: for of Him comes my salvation" (Ps. 62.1).

Perhaps you may ask how does one become still and shut out the things we have just been doing or about to do, or the concerns and worries of our work and life? The world has become a noisy place and so silence in our noisy world is like the sunshine after a severe thunderstorm, or like a port for a vessel which has been tossed around on the turbulent sea. Noise, even music, is an awful distraction and irritation when we want to still the soul. Having somewhere quiet and restful is most helpful and that is why before the Tabernacle in church is an obvious place. However we are not all in the position of attending daily Mass, and even if we do, the day came be almost over. So another time and place have to be made. It may help some if I suggest what seems to work for me.

Setting time aside each day when I am fresh is important and thus I make my main meditative and contemplative time first thing

---

14 Anselm, p. 239.
15 Gore, *Oracle*, p. 19.

in the morning after having my cup of tea. It is a new day which the Lord has made, with new hopes and adventures, and any problems of yesterday are shelved or in the words of the early Fathers we guard against "morning demons" which want to poison the day by yesterday's worries. By having my cuppa, it gives me time to awaken properly. I then meditate on the readings for Mass that day, and offer up prayers from these readings. By this stage I find my being has begun to tune in as it were to that other country. I am stilled. I am now ready, either kneeling or sitting, to be quiet, to acknowledge God's presence within me and let Him take over. Of course there are times when I find my mind wondering, and my concentration falters, and I lose that perfect stillness, but as I kneel/sit in front of an icon, by opening my eyes and fixing on it, and perhaps offering up the Jesu prayer simultaneously, it helps me to stillness again. At this point I have now moved into the next stage of the spiritual life, the contemplative, or tapping "the cloud unknowing". I shall leave writing about that for another day.

The important thing to remember is until we give ourselves the opportunity to learn to still ourselves, we can never utter that prayer of the child Samuel, "Speak Lord, for your servant hears" or hear that small voice which came to Elijah in his hour of need. That gave him the strength to carry out Yahweh's work.

The key word to practice stillness is perseverance. There are many times when we don't achieve a quiet stillness or harmony within ourselves. Don't despair, but do consider that Satan does not want us to be at one with God, and he will place many temptations before us in order to woo us away from Him. We therefore must simply not give up! Remember those wandering thoughts or shuffles can be turned into prayer. This should bring us back to God and His presence. Persevere this Lent and if your parish has regular Exposition of the Sacrament take the opportunity to kneel and be still in the Lord's presence. It is the best way I know of for growing closer to our dear Saviour and to hear His words, "Follow me."

Lord you often withdrew from the crowds for a place of quietness to pray to Your Father. Teach me how to be still so I can hear Your voice calling, "Follow me." Amen.

FIRST SUNDAY IN LENT

TEMPTATION

*Then was Jesus led up of the Spirit
into the wilderness to be tempted of
the devil.*

Matthew 4. 1.

Full Readings:

Cycle A: Genesis 2. 7-9, 3. 1-7; Psalm 51; Romans 5.12-19; Matthew 4.1-11.

Cycle B: Genesis 9. 8- 15; Psalm 25; 1 Peter 3.18-27; Mark 1. 12-15.

Cycle C: Deuteronomy 26. 4-10; Psalm 91. 1-2, 10-15; Romans 10.8-13; Luke 4. 1-13.

EVERY YEAR ON THE first Sunday in Lent we hear the account of our Lord's temptation in the wilderness as the Gospel for the day, and perhaps familiarity breeds contempt. As we have heard it so many, many times we feel we know it all, and we can become rather indifferent to it. Yet our Saviour's struggle with the devil, and facing similar temptations of the world as we do, should make us realize this Lent that He has identified Himself with us in our temptations. During Lent the devil is going to tempt us many times as we try to keep our resolutions and set our face towards Jerusalem to walk with Christ during His last week. The devil is very clever, but if we keep before us our Lord's forty days, it is possible to say, as Jesus did, "Get thee behind me Satan".

Andrewes in one of his sermon on our Lord's temptations, encourages us to "go out into the wilderness ... [to] mark how our Saviour wards and defends Himself" so that "we may be armed with the same mind" when tempted. Nevertheless "since the devil spared not to tempt our Saviour, he will be much more bold with us." After all "if he ... sought our overthrow in Christ, how much more will he do it in ourselves?" For certain "it is the devil's occupation to defame us first with God", and then "God with us." It was "his defaming God with us [which] was the cause of all sin; and everywhere still he laboureth to persuade us that God is an unkind God." The fact that Satan pursued Christ into the desert only illustrates for us "that there is no place privileged from temptations. ... There is no place so holy, no exercise so good, as can repress his courage, or give a stay to the boldness of his attempts."[16]

Of course we are not going to be like Christ and be victorious over Satan every time we are tempted. We are going to sin, but that is why we have the sacrament of Confession. We know He will be compassionate towards us providing we are penitent. The important factor is to admit our failures and then start afresh. We can also derive comfort from knowing that our Lord, because He has Himself being tempted, knows "how strong the 'assailant was who thrust sore at Him that He might fall', and how feeble our nature is to make resistance." It is also reassuring that when we are tempted, "He leads us by the hand, and stands by as a faithful assistant." He is ever there to strengthen us, we but have to ask![17] We should also recall God's words to Cain before he killed his brother, "sin is lurking at the door, its desire is for you, but you must master it" (Gen. 4.7).

Another thought worth contemplating on this day is, that as we capitulate to our temptations so often, it should make us more compassionate towards our brethren's weaknesses and sins, or what we consider their weaknesses and sins. God may not have the same opinion! After all there by the grace of God, go I!

How often should I forgive my brethren their trespasses? "Till seventy times," was our Lord's reply. We have to remember if we see a speck in our brethren's eye, that we have a beam within ours. Quite a difference! It is a sobering thought for Lent. Let us be patient with the sins of others, as we too are sinners, but hopefully penitent sinners.

---

16 Andrewes, Vol.5, pp. 480 - 2, 494.
17 Ibid., pp. 485 - 6.

Finally remember that Satan lost the battle against our dear Lord. He does not have to win with us either!

My dearest Saviour, in my times of temptations let me be mindful of Your victory over Satan, and Your desire for me to resist him. Make me truly sorry when I fail You and give me resolve to start afresh. Amen.

SIN

You shall not steal; neither deal falsely,
neither lie one to another.

Leviticus 19. 11.

Full Readings: Leviticus 19.1-2, 11-18; Psalm 19. 8-15; Matthew 25.31-46.

BOTH READINGS FROM LEVITICUS and the Gospel to-day confront us with the reality of sin when we do not fulfil the commandment of love towards our brothers and sisters as Christ has taught us. Not carrying out that commandment has serious repercussions.

Yesterday we spoke about temptation and when we open the door to it we sin. Let us to-day focus on sin. The first thing we must remember is that sin is not of God's creation. Everything God created is good and so sin is outside His nature. In man's primal state he did not know sin, but when he disobeyed God, "his eyes were open" and in that instance he knew both "good and evil". Thus sin is contrary to God's nature, and is therefore evil. Andrewes put it very succinctly, "sin ... will destroy us all," while Mother Julian tells us that "sin is the sharpest scourge that any chosen soul can be smitten with."[18] We know that Christ died for our sins, but how often do we realize that He also died for us to cease from sin and to be free of that slavery. Thus when we sin we are allowing ourselves to be enslaved by it. Christ beckons us to realize our potential to rise above such bondage. Andrewes assured us that the whole purpose of God's nativity was to take "upon Him the shape of man" with this end in mind "to save

---

18 Andrewes, Vol. 1, p. 74; Julian of Norwich, p. 124.

soul and body from the bodily and ghostly enemies; from sin the root, and misery the branches, for a time and for ever," in order that "He might restore the work of God to His original perfection", that is, above sin.[19] We are called to be Easter people!

Nevertheless we all do sin, and sin often, despite our efforts of trying to conquer it and live a life of holiness. When we sin there is no point in being morbid about it, and letting the thought of being a miserable sinner dominate our lives. Rather the Christian response is to be sorry for it, confess and acknowledge it, ask God's forgiveness and help not to sin again and then to get on with living in the spirit of the Resurrection. Again Mother Julian reminds us that "Our courteous Lord [does not want] his servants [to] despair for often failing" most grievously. He wants us to know that "He is the ground of ... our whole life in love, and furthermore that He is our everlasting keeper and mightily defends us against all our enemies" who attack us.[20]

If we do not acknowledge and confess our sins what happens? It means we separate ourselves from God and estrange ourselves from the channels of grace. Julian once again reminds us that even "the pains of hell, purgatory, earth, [and] death" are more preferable to be endured than sin. "For sin is so vile and so hateful, that no pain we experience can ever compare with it."[21] Sin of course affects our spiritual life. How can we pray? How can we love? How can we live in peace with ourselves? Even receiving the Sacrament is to our damnation and not to our comfort. Sin simply pollutes and sours everything in life, and prevents us from attaining that "sovereign good". "By selling ourselves over to sin and Satan, we have put ourselves out of our own; into their dominion; and (during that state) remain wholly to be disposed at their pleasure."[22]

Sometimes we try to convince ourselves it was but a little sin and therefore of little consequence. Even little sins are like worms which eventually devour our souls. In truth all sins are equal. Taylor indicated this when he insisted, "all sins are single in their acting, and both *great* and *small* are under the same danger. ... Between sins great and little, actual and habitual, there is no difference of nature or formality, but only of degrees."[23]

---

19 Andrewes, Vol. 1, p. 79, Vol. 5, p. 479.
20 Julian of Norwich, pp. 126-7.
21 Ibid., p. 129.
22 Sanderson, Vol. 2, p. 168.
23 Taylor, Vol. 7, pp. 134 - 5.

When we do confront our sins and acknowledge them, it enables us to see ourselves as God sees us. This confrontation strips us and makes us naked not only before God but also gives us self-knowledge; we become aware of ourselves as we truly are. There is no pretence and superficiality to living. We have to become naked in order to be clothed with His righteousness. Yet at the same time we are freed, liberated from the tyranny of sin.

Lent is the time to consider whether sin has a grip on us, or whether we have a grip on it. If the former we need to do something about it. Repent. That is the subject in a couple days.

Dear Lord, help me to be early in my repenting, so that I may never be separated from Your love and presence for long. Strengthen me with Your sweet and divine grace to fight against sin and to continue being Your faithful servant unto my life's end. Amen.

Ejaculatory Prayer

When you pray, use not vain repetitions,
as the heathens do; for they think they
will be heard for their much speaking.

Matthew 6. 7.

Full Readings: Isaiah 55. 10-11; Psalm 34. 4-7, 16-9; Matthew 6.7-15.

PRAYER FOR THE SOUL is like water for the earth, as the prophet reminds us this morning in the reading from Isaiah. Without it the soil is parched. Today I want to talk about a special kind of prayer, ejaculatory prayer. The Psalmist articulates, "Let my prayer be set forth in your sight as the incense" (Ps.141.2). Paul reminds us to pray without ceasing and Christ teaches us, as He did to His disciples, to be simple in our praying. Ejaculatory or arrow prayers, as they are sometimes called, allow us to do all that. They are short and can be offered up to the Father as often as we like. Let me explain. Sometimes these prayers are just one word, such as "Jesu", "Jesus", "Lord" and even "help"; sometimes they are a short sentence such as "My God I you adore", "Lord have mercy", and "Comfort me with your Spirit". They can also be longer especially when we want to pray during the day for a particular person or situation. The list is endless and at the end I shall give more examples.

Ejaculatory prayers when practised frequently are almost spontaneously. You will discover this Lent if you are trying to live the Christian life that God becomes not an absentee landlord but a tenant who lives with you. You grow in recognizing that He is always there,

22

and like having a friend staying with you there are times when you want to converse with Him in petition and praise. These become our arrow prayers.

Arrow prayers cover all spectra, just as our conversations with our friends do. When we desperately need guidance in a situation, we instinctively pray, "Help!", whether we recognize it as a prayer or not; sometimes we may be more polite and say, "Dear Lord help me." When out walking or cycling on a gorgeous morning we find ourselves exclaiming, "How glorious is your world;" or "Thank you for such a smashing day."

Many a time our small acts of self-denials are offered with such prayers: "This is to praise Your name, dear Lord," or "I do this as an act of love to You, my Saviour," or, "This is for Peter who is lonely" or something similar. While listening to the news we also can offer ejaculatory prayer by commending that situation into His hands, or lifting up that person before His presence. Then there are just the ordinary times when we reach out and declare, "I know you are there."

As mentioned above, one ejaculatory prayer is simply saying the holy name, "Jesus" or "Jesu". This Jesu prayer, known as the prayer of the heart, has been practised by Christians for centuries and is uttered with much adoration and devotion. It is a very special kind of arrow prayer as it is often repeated over and over again to bring the soul into one with God. In the Western Church the name of Jesus is invoked on it own. However in the Eastern Church it is mostly a whole sentence, "Lord Jesus Christ, Son of David have mercy on me." A monk of the Eastern Church in explaining how to pray this prayer advised that firstly "all tension and haste must be avoided". The goal "is not a constant liberal repetition but a kind of latent presence of the names of Jesus in our hearts." Secondly, begin to pronounce it with "loving adoration. ... Cling to it, and repeat it slowly, gently and quietly." As you do this, do not think that you are invoking the name; but think only of Jesus Himself. As you practise this often you will soon find that the name of Jesus will come spontaneously to your lips and almost continually be present in your mind, even in the subconscious.[24]

As suggested repeating this holy name has also been associated with showing great adoration to Jesus, fittingly expressed by the me-

---

24   *The Prayer of Jesus*, pp. 98 - 9.

dievalist mystic, Richard Rolle, in offering counsel to a female recipi-
ent, but also sound advice to us during this Lent:

> May [I] love your name Jesus, and meditate on it in my heart,
> so that I may never forget it wherever I am. I shall find great joy
> and strength in your name, Lord Jesus, and because I love you
> so tenderly, and as such an intimate friend, You will fill me with
> grace on this earth.
> Rolle urged her and us to:
> Pray that you do desire to be God's lover, you do love His name
> Jesus, and ponder it in your heart, so that you do not forget it
> never, wheresoever you are. And truly I tell you that you will
> find much joy and comfort therein. And for the love wherewith
> you love Jesus, so tenderly and so specially, you will be filled full
> of grace on earth and be Christ's maiden and spouse in heav-
> en.[25]

It is also the prayer on the lips of those in terrible pain and agony.
It is indeed their source of strength and comfort when the only physical reality is pain piercing their very being, and thus any other kind
of prayer is almost impossible. Those of us who have experienced excruciating pain in our lives know this only too well. The Jesu prayer
is the lifeline.

This Lent, if you have not discovered Jesus as a friend, find
Him. Make up your own ejaculatory prayers. The Psalms are a good
source, and most of the ejaculatory prayers included here are based
on excerpts from the Psalms.

- I adore You, dear Lord, help me to love You more and more.
- Holy God, holy and mighty, holy and immortal, have mercy
  upon us.
- Lord have mercy.
- Jesus you are my all.
- The heavens and earth are full of your glory.
- I praise You O God.
- Praise the Lord, O my soul.

---

25 Rolle, p. 94.

- O give thanks unto the Lord for He is gracious and His mercy endures for ever.

- The darkness is no darkness with Thee.

- Lord, You have searched me out, and known me.

- Your loving kindness and mercy will follow me all the days of my life.

- My soul does magnify the Lord.

- Forgive me dear Lord.

- Blessed be the name of the Lord.

- Your work is worthy to be praised, and had in honour.

- I shall lift up my eyes unto the hills, from whence comes my help.

- My help comes from the Lord who has made heaven and earth.

- The Lord will preserve me from all evil.

- The Lord Himself is my keeper.

- The earth is the Lord's, and all therein is.

- You know me so well, that my faults are never hidden from You, O Lord.

- Create in me a clean heart O God, and renew a right spirit within me.

- I acknowledge my faults and my sins are ever before me.

My dear Lord may Your holy name be constantly on my lips as a source of comfort and strength. Teach me to recognize your presence throughout the day. Amen.

REPENTANCE

The men of Nineveh ... repented
at the preaching of Jonas.

Luke 11. 32.

Full Readings: Jonah 3. 1-10; Psalm 51.3- 4, 12-3, 18-9; Luke 11.29-32.

THE BOOK OF JONAH tells of that prophet's preaching to the king and people of Nineveh about their sinful ways, and consequently God would destroy the city in forty days. However both king and his people heeded Jonah's warning and repented of their sins in sackcloth and ashes and so God spared their city. Unlike the Ninevites the Israelites never responded to the warnings from their prophets such as Jeremiah and Ezekiel of the consequences of their forsaking God and their other sins. The latter had proclaimed "'Repent, and turn yourselves from all your transgressions; so iniquity shall not be your ruin'" (Ez.18.30). As a result the Israelites were taken into captivity, and although some of them sat down by the waters of Babylon and wept it did not do them any good for many years.

As the Ninevites showed, repentance means being contrite for sins and making a fresh and new way of living, that is, entirely different from how they had previously lived. It is a turning away from sin and turning to God (*metanoia*). As Taylor expressed it, we "must not suffer anything to remain behind which may ever spring up and bear the apples of Sodom."[26] Repentance also involves making God the centre of our lives and not ourselves; we wish to take the "i" out

---

26 Taylor, Vol. 7, p. 418.

of "sin". More than that, we wish to live with God every moment of our lives.

If this is our desire, then repentance is something we practise daily, even hourly if necessary. "Not to repent instantly, is a great loss of our time, and it may for ought we know become the loss of all our hopes."[27] With repentance comes relief and its own reward, when we have decided to do something about our sins against God and man. Hooker described this reward as:

> A recovery of the soul of man from deadly sickness, a restitution of glorious light to his darkened mind, a comfortable reconciliation with God, a spiritual nativity, a rising from the dead, a dayspring from out the depth of obscurity, ... a full restoration of the seat of grace and throne of glory, a triumph over sin, and a saving victory.[28]

The imposition of ashes on our foreheads on Ash Wednesday is a sober reminder that our life here is fleeting, and the Church certainly does not advocate death-bed repentance as a surety to heaven. We should always live in preparation for death. This is why the Caroline Divines so often preached on the urgency of repentance with much emphasis on *metanioa*. Accordingly Andrewes stated firstly, "look forward to God, and with our 'whole heart' resolve to 'turn' to Him", and secondly to "look backward to our sins wherein we have turned from God". Thus in this "turning" there are two distinct parts: "One, conversion from sin; [and] the other contrition for sin. One resolving to amend [what] is to come, the other reflecting and sorrowing for [what] is past. One declining from evil to be done hereafter, the other sentencing itself for evil done heretofore." Both of these Andrewes warned are needed for "a complete repentance", without which we cannot begin to grow in the Christian life[29]. This Divine is of course so right when he stated this may be our last Lent, it may even be our last day. None of us has a guarantee against sudden death. Repentance therefore should act as a constant and sober reminder that our earthly pilgrimage is but fleeting, just as Lent itself reminds us, now is the time for repenting of our sins.

---

27 Ibid., p. 154.
28 Hooker, Vol. 3, p. 62.
29 Andrewes, Vol. 1, p. 359.

Therefore repentance is the one aspect of life we can never shelve. It is crucial for Christian living and dying. It is the heart of the Gospel as illustrated by both the teaching of the Baptist and Christ. Unlike the other Gospel writers Mark began his with John's words to repent. So let us repent for the kingdom of heaven is at hand this Lent.

Dear Saviour, You came into this world to make men whole and for them to realize their full potential, give me Your grace to aspire always towards this. When I sin and blemish my potential, make me repent quickly and turn back to You with a contrite heart. Amen.

Intercessory Prayer

'Ask, and it will be given to you …
For everyone who asks will receive.'

Matthew 7. 7 - 8.

Full Readings: Esther 14. 1- 7; Psalm 138. 1-8; Matthew 7.7 -12.

Our Lord has assured us in today's Gospel reading, if we approach Him in faith Christ will hear our supplications, and intercede on our behalf. Since His Ascension Christ is our High Priest in heaven whom we can approach with boldness (Heb. 4.14). He is thus continually pleading to His Father on our behalf. That is why we end our prayers "through Christ our Lord". Catholic Christians further believe that Our Lady, the saints and the faithful who now live in the nearer presence of God also intercede to Christ for us. So when we pray for others each day, we are joining our intercessory prayers with this heavenly network. Mother Julian expresses this all so delightfully when she spoke of our Lord in heaven, after accepting our prayers, puts them in the treasury where it will never perish. "It is there before God, with all his holy saints" and where it speedily receives "our needs". The wonderful news about this is that when we reach heaven it will be "given [to] us, for a degree of joy." Here our worship will be ceaseless, ever thanking Him that "with his grace [He] makes us like unto Himself."[30]

For whom should we pray? (Esther prayed for her people's deliverance from the new decree). Obviously we cannot pray for every

---

30 Julian of Norwich, p. 133.

person and every situation which needs praying for each day. Some people arrange their intercessory prayers under various headings or themes for each day of the week. For instance on one day of the week, prayers revolve around the handicapped, the afflicted, poor, homeless, unemployed and social rejects. And on another for all those who work to protect our society and so on. Some pray according to the needs of each day that flow from the readings of the day and current events. I tend to do this.

We are also bound to pray for specific people and to offer them up into God's loving care. Again some have a set pattern for this: one day for family members, another for specific friends, and yet another for the sick. Some parishes, including my own, allow intercessions from the gathered for daily Mass at the end of the General Intercessions. This is a wonderful opportunity to pray for those especially in need of daily prayer. Another practical time for intercessory prayer is at Exposition of the Sacrament.

Some of us belong to a prayer chain and regularly pray for all those on the prayer list and those needing instant prayer via a 'phone call. Another way is to pray for people when we visit or communicate with them by letter or 'phone. Irrespective of how we pray for those in need, God knows our prayers before we ask; nevertheless He wants us to ask. In every matter "let your requests be made known unto God" (Col.4.6).

How often should we pray for a particular person? Do we pray over and over and over each day for someone who is seriously ill for example? No, I don't think this is necessary. When a close friend is ill or for someone who has particularly asked for our prayers what I think we should do at the beginning of each day is to commend the particular person(s) to God and ask Him to do His will in him/her and leave it as that. One of my favourite prayers is for God to make a particular person the person He wants him/her to be and for His will to be done. God knows that you desire the friend to be healed or whatever, and He will do that, but in His own way. Part of intercessory prayer is to trust our heavenly Father.

However we arrange our intercessions it is a vital part of praying each day. If this is a neglected aspect of our praying use this Lent to compile your own intercessory prayer book. For each day of the week jot down those people, organizations and situations you would like to include in your prayers. Don't make it too long as that can tempt us to rattle them off rather than placing each before God prayerfully. Furthermore always leave time for the spontaneity of the Holy Spirit to probe our memory.

Our intercessions cement our relationship with our fellow Christians within Christ's community throughout the world. We know that as we pray for Christ's world, other Christians are doing likewise. The sun never ceases on prayer. Heaven and earth are one in this ceaseless act of intercession, and will be so until the last day.

Dear Father, You are always ready to hear our prayers. Help me to see the needs of our world and for its people and offer them up to You through Your beloved Son. Amen.

CONFESSION

When the wicked man turns away from his wickedness
... and does what is lawful and right, he shall save his soul.

Ezekiel 18. 27.

Full Readings: Ezekiel 18. 21-28; Psalm 130. 1-8; Matthew 5. 20 –26.

INTERWOVEN WITH REPENTANCE IS confession. Whereas repentance is feeling and thinking sorrow for our sins, confession is the actual admission and enumerating of what those sins are. George Herbert expressed it:

> Lord I confess my sin is great;
> Great is my sin. ...
> I do confess
> My foolishness:
> My God, accept of my confession.[31]

We can never cloak our sins from God, and therefore making a confession involves a thorough searching of our souls so that we can be honest with God and ourselves. As we delve into the way we have lived each day, we soon discover how we have sinned against God, others and even ourselves. That is why it is important to make a daily self examination of our lives at the end of each day.

Confession is essential to live in tune with God, that is, a life of holiness. Catholic Christians regularly use the sacrament of Con-

---

31 Dorman, pp. 41-2.

fession/Reconciliation for confessing their sins. The latter name indicates the heart of confession as indicated in today's Gospel: "Be reconciled with your brother before bringing your gift to the altar" and of course with God. For those who have never confessed their sins through this sacrament, let me assure you it is surrounded with much joy and peace. Of course it is not something which we find easy, no matter how many times we have used this sacrament; but because we know the joys of the surety of God's forgiveness through the absolution pronounced by the priest in His name, we thank God for it. The sacrament of Confession also helps us to grieve more ardently for our sins, and to amend our lives more assuredly. Thus when we leave the confessional, we are resolute to sin no more. It is a wonderful feeling to walk away from the confessional knowing that God has truly forgiven. It is like a taste of what heaven must be like, be it only a moment. If only we could linger there and not succumb to sin again. Oh, this frail flesh, but temporarily forgotten in the joy of the moment!

Once we have ascertained the therapeutic and spiritual worth of confessing our sins before a priest, what is actually involved in doing that? Sparrow tells us for "a true confession" we must firstly "accuse ourselves, not laying the blame on others; [secondly], it must be ... with grief and sorrow for them; [thirdly], we must confess all our sins we know, not willingly concealing any; [and fourthly], with a purpose of obedience for the time to come."[32]

Perhaps you may ask what constitutes a sin? There are two kinds: mortal and venial. The former includes murder, adultery and stealing while the latter includes impatience, bad temper, judging and not loving others. I find using passages of Scripture such as the Beatitudes, Paul's list of the fruits of the spirit and the attributes of love the best way to prepare for confession. Firstly, we invoke the Holy Spirit to direct the examination of our souls before reading the selected passage of Scripture. The Spirit will help to scrutinize our lives against the text. Jot down those sins which come to mind in preparation for making our confession.

Of course little purpose is achieved in making our confession unless we are resolved not to sin again and to make a sterling stab at it. We know "we have dishonoured Him by our sins, so we must en-

---

32 Sparrow, p. 5.

deavour a restitution, and glorify him by our good works," Sparrow taught.[33] Today's Gospel reading makes it clear that we must live in charity with our neighbours before we can worship God at the altar. To help us to fight against sin, we should keep before us, as often as possible a picture of a crucifix as this is the cost of our sins. Ask yourself, do I really desire to drive those nails any further into His hands and feet through my habitual sinning? Remember, "to repent is to leave a sin"; and to wish one "had never done the sin."[34]

Another advantage of making use of sacramental confession regularly is the counselling and help one receives from the confessor. We have the opportunity to speak to him about those besetting sins, and any other spiritual problems. A spiritual Father becomes a dear friend. So perhaps this Lent is a good time to start this habit, if not already. I am sure you will find your parish priest willing to help you make your first confession. Psychiatrists as well as priests will tell you that confession is good for the soul; it has always been accepted as being one of the outlets for healthy living. Just one other point - your spiritual mentor does not need to be your priest, or even a priest. There are many laymen/women who also make good spiritual directors. The important thing is to have one to monitor our spiritual lives.

Dear God give me an honest heart to see my sins as You see them and to confess them humbly and sincerely. May Your loving Spirit help me to grow in holiness so that I may be Yours for ever. Amen.

---

33 Ibid., p. 13.
34 Taylor, Vol. 7, pp. 424, 433.

LOVE

I say unto you, Love your enemies, …
and pray for those who … persecute you.

Matthew 5. 44.

Full Readings: Deuteronomy 26.16-19; Psalm 119. 1-2, 4-5, 7-8; Matthew 5. 43-48.

TOWARDS THE END OF Lent I shall write about loving God. Today I shall concentrate on love as it should be lived out by Christians, as evident in to-day's Gospel reading. Love is the most powerful and positive thing in the world; it is "the noblest passion and highest felicity which the soul is capable of in this, or the life to come," stated the devout seventeenth century layman, John Evelyn.[35] As Christ taught, it is the essence of Christianity while the Johannine letters stressed that we cannot truly love God if we do not love the person with whom we live and work. In their sermons the Caroline Divines also made no bones about it. Shelford preached, "There is nothing that makes man more like to God than love" while Farindon declared, "If I do not love [my brethren], I shall hate my own soul; and whose salvation if I do not seriously tender, I shall forfeit my own."[36]

Yet at times it is also the most difficult thing to do, even after we have prayed to be able to love a particular person. How can we love that person whose very habits pierce the sensitivity of our souls? We all have people in our lives with whom we have great difficulty in

---

35 Evelyn, p. 12.
36 Shelford, pp. 98, 112; Farindon, Vol. 3, p. 399.

loving. For me it is domineering people who want to be in charge of everything and can never let be. A good priest friend of mine suggests that when we find it hard to love someone, let us always act as love should. If we act as love should, then we shall indeed feel love. It is the love that St. Francis showed when he embraced the leper on that lonely Umbrian road. Love means reaching out, and touching and embracing.

What must we do to embrace our leper? Firstly we have to expose ourselves as much as possible to God's love. That is why for me being present at the daily Eucharist is crucial. I know without Christ I am a frail shell, but here "Love [bids] me welcome" and Love gives Himself to me. "If Love carry us to the Lover of souls, we cannot come too often to this Holy Table."[37] Having Love within me, and being assured of God's love to every creature, I can start afresh of telling myself that God loves this person very much and he/she is very precious to Him. He/she is made in the image of God, and to deny that person love is to deny Christ. That helps tremendously.

Secondly, praying when you find the situation almost intolerable is also positive. Try to place that person in God's loving hands and out of your own. The prayer which I find helpful is our Lord's prayer from the cross, "Father forgive them, for they know not what they do." A person can be quiet unaware of the effect he/she has upon another, while on the other hand the other lacks the perception to acknowledge this. Lastly, lay it at the foot of the cross, offer it up and try to leave it there. Once that has been done, it is possible to see the person rather than the irritability and to see him/her as Christ's child too. Then we can give ourselves a chance to love. At such times of irritability I am quite aware that one often feels more like walking away or shouting, but I can assure you if you make yourself pray it does work many times. The other positive reflection at such times is that giving in to our irritability shows that we are lacking the self-discipline that in a sense we are criticizing and we are letting down Christ. That sobers one!

The sensual is also very important in loving others. Our eyes convey our feelings very much (not only love and warmth, but alas hatred, anger and indifference) and that is why eye contact is always essential in conversation. You must look at the person to whom you

---

37 Dorman, p. 29; Evelyn, p. 12.

are speaking. I am sure you are aware how awful it is to speak to another person who never looks at you, and what a demoralizing affect it has! Yet it is in our touching another person that we probably convey the most warmth and love. Our skins are very sensitive, and when one reaches out, and takes another person's hand or puts an arm around a person love is communicated. Often touching are our words. Thus for those nearest to us, but hardest to love, learn to put a hand on the shoulder. It says so much, and you will be amazed at what it does for you!

Hammond reminded us that love is the heart of the Gospel. "Christ's design in this life [is] to set up charity, friendship above all virtues, as high as it is above all felicities, [and] to settle that for prime Christian duty." Furthermore "love of my brother's virtues, love of his soul; love of the nature that Christ assumed and died for, and carried to heaven with him; love of the image of God in him [has] that most transporting durable pleasure."[38]

We must remember the opposite from loving is living in hell because hell is the only place exclusive of love. Thus for Christians there is only one course, and that of course is to love and to love unconditionally. We know this will bring frustrations, disappointments, rejections, tears and our heart will break into many pieces very often, and sometimes it will be agonizing to pick up those pieces. That is the risk we take and of course living out the Christian life is a risky business. The comfort is that our dear Saviour has already been there. No heart shattered as His did as He looked upon the world from His cross.

Dear Lord, You came amongst us so that the loveless might lovely be, help me through Your Holy Spirit to embrace those I find loveless. Make them as lovely to me as they are in Your sight. Amen.

---

38 Hammond, Vol. 1, p. 38.

TRANSFORMATION

Jesus was transfigured before them.

Matthew 17. 2.

Full Readings:

Cycle A: Genesis 12.1-4a; Psalm 33; 2 Timothy 1.8-10; Matthew 17.2.

Cycle B: Genesis 22. 1-2, 9-13, 15-18; Psalm 115; Romans 8. 31-4; Mark 9. 2.10.

Cycle C: Genesis 15. 5-12, 17-18; Psalm 27. 1, 7-9, 13-14; Philippians 3.17- 4.1; Luke 9. 28-36.

THE GOSPEL READING FOR to-day is the Transfiguration when our Lord is shown in all His glory before the inner three on Mount Tabor. It is a foretaste of what is to come, but not before Christ has to suffer and die. Just as Christ was transfigured on the mount so our lives should gradually be transformed through the Holy Spirit.

We are called to a life of holiness, and by that I don't mean living away from the world. For some peculiar reason holiness has been equated with forsaking the world as it is seen as luring us into all kinds of fleshly and spiritual sins. Yet the pursuit of holiness does not come from running away but from facing reality. So our Christian life must be one of growth, growing away from self and towards God or in other words taking to heart the words of John Baptist, "He must increase, but I must decrease" (Jn 3.30). Then we are gradually being transformed from the old self in Adam to the new self in Christ. As we grow away from self we become more aware not only of our God given potential but also of the world's tarnish through man's sins. As

St. Paul expressed it, "the whole creation has been groaning in labour pain" (Rom. 8.22). Nevertheless God is still present in His creation.

Consequently growing in holiness means we interact with the world despite the atrocities and the grief it causes. The misuse of God's world can only be redirected by His working through us, and therefore we must be His hands and feet and spokesmen. Being holy will often mean doing and saying things which are unpopular. For example we must advocate peace rather than warfare as He is the Prince of Peace; condemn greed and try to have it redirected in order to feed the poor as Christ taught; advocate the right to life from the moment of conception as God is the giver of all life; and involve ourselves with the poor and the needy. Holiness is nothing less than following Christ's example.

To have a sanctifying approach to our world means that our inward lives have to grow in holiness. After all we can only manifest what is part of our very being. Our transformation into holiness is of course the working of the Holy Spirit. That means having time in prayer, stillness and contemplation so that we can empty ourselves of self-centredness and breathe in God. We get to know God a little better in every prayer time we have, and so we can recognize Him more distinctly in His world.

Holiness also has nothing to do with being pretentious and posing piously but it has everything to do about being natural and ourselves. So it does not mean we go around with sobered faces and being judgmental of others. In accepting ourselves as we are, we can then accept others as they are and use this as the basis for the work we do in His name. Holiness means that we grow in those virtues which are characteristic in a life of holiness such as humility and love, patience and tolerance, forgiving and forbearing.

Perhaps too our habits at Mass need transforming to help us grow in holiness. Do we arrive in time to kneel and pray and recollect our thoughts? Could we reflect more on the readings beforehand so that they are more meaningful when we hear them during the Liturgy of the Word? Could we participate more fully by making our responses more definite? Could we be more reverent in our approach and receiving the Sacrament? Could we give a more heartfelt thanksgiving afterwards to our blessed Saviour?

Each one of us is called to this life of holiness simply because that is fulfilling the creative, redemptive and sanctifying work of the

Trinity. Otherwise God's purpose for us is thwarted and we diminish that operation of the divine within and we become a shadow of what we were meant to be.

Lent is the perfect time to have our lives transformed and one of the best reflections for this is on our dear Lady's life. How her life must have been transformed by following her Son during His ministry as she gradually came to realise who He is and what would be ahead of Him. Her presence in the upper room in Jerusalem with the disciples awaiting the promise of the coming of the Holy Spirit manifests how much she had been transformed.

O Holy Spirit, teach me that holiness demands living out Your Gospel in all situations in this world, however difficult. Let me be Your instrument of peace, love and reconciliation in a world torn by hatred, greed and violence. Amen.

MERCY

To the Lord our God belong mercies and forgivenesses.
Daniel 9. 9.

Full Readings: Daniel 9. 4-10; Psalm 79. 8-13; Luke 6. 26 – 8.

GOD'S MERCY KNOWS NO bounds yet in a real sense the only demand we can make on God is for mercy, His infinite mercy. Like Daniel and also the Psalmist we can say "My trust is in the tender mercy of God for ever and ever" (Ps. 52.9). Our human nature is fraught with frailty, fragility and failure. That is why the ejaculatory prayers, "Lord have mercy", and the longer one, "Holy God, Holy and mighty, Holy and immortal, have mercy upon us", are often on the lips of Christians. We constantly implore His mercy for the many times we fail Him and stab His wounded side. As Shakespeare expressed it, "The quality of mercy is not strained/ It droppeth as the gentle rain from heaven/ Upon the place beneath."[39] It is indeed most wonderful news for Christians to know that this mercy drops from heaven and that God is always there waiting to be merciful and forgiving. His mercy flows from His love where "in heaven ... His mercies are ever in their maturity." Donne explained there has never been a time when there was not mercy as "God has had such a care of all men" that He always puts "mercy before judgment" as His mercy is greater than all the atoms of the air. "His mercy has no relation to time, no limitation in time, it is not first, nor last, but eternal, everlasting." Indeed:

---

39 Shakespeare, p. 69.

Begin where you will at any act in yourself, at any act in God,
yet there was mercy before that, for His mercy is eternal, eternal even towards you. ... Earth cannot receive, heaven cannot
give such another universal soul to all: all persons, all actions,
as mercy. And were I the child ... who were to live an hundred
years, I would ask no other marrow to my bones, no other wine
to my heart, no other light to my eyes, no other art to my understanding, no other eloquence to my tongue, than the power of
apprehending for myself, and the power of deriving and con-
veying upon others by my ministry, the mercy, the early mercy,
the everlasting mercy of yours, and my God.[40]

Mother Julian assured us too that mercy is the work of God's
goodness, and "it will last working as long as sin is suffered to pursue rightful souls."[41]

Whenever we celebrate the major Christian festivals, God's mercy is clearly abundant. The greatest mercy is of course celebrated at
the joyous festival of Christmas when God became man for our salvation. This in turns means "that God and I shall never be parted".
That merciful act of Christ was sealed on the cross and given fruition
at Pentecost.

Perhaps there are times when God's mercy seems hidden from
us, or we feel we do not deserve to seek God's forgiveness and mercy.
Once again Donne assures us that at such times "the mercy of God
may slumber [and] ... be hidden from His servants, but it cannot be
taken away, and in the greatest necessities, it will break out."[42] Indeed the fact that God has told us about hell "is ... a monument ... of
His mercy" because if we were not warned about it, "we should all
fall into [it]."[43]

Knowing that God is always more ready to be merciful than being judgemental towards us, it should mean we reciprocate this in
our Christian living with others. Being judgmental is the easy way
out. It is much easier to be merciless than merciful, but it also breeds
contempt, pride, and anger which work against the Holy Spirit. Being merciful on the other hand involves love, understanding and
commitment, but it also leads to tenderness and gentleness. Then our

40 Donne, *Fifty Sermons*, p. 222.
41 Julian of Norwich, p. 112.
42 Donne, *Eighty Sermons*, p. 14.
43 Ibid., p. 263.

mercy is "most pure and clear without taint or trouble." Indeed "love opens the fountain, or rather [is] the fountain from whence it flows, when the love of Christ has begot in us the love of our brethren, and we show mercy to them ... for Christ's sake," declared Farindon.[44]

Just as God's mercy springs from His love for His frail creatures, so too must our mercy flow from our love of God and our fellow man. Farindon further challenges us with this question, "Will [mercy] be a jewel in every cabinet but your own hearts?" "The proper act of mercy is to flow and to spend itself, and yet not to be spent; to relieve our brethren in misery, and in all the degrees that lead to it. ... To part with our coat to our brother is as necessary now as when Christ first taught it." This Divine assures us that "God's mercy is ready to shine upon ours, for He loves it, and loves to look on it."[45] This Lent practise being as merciful as Your heavenly Father is, knowing that it is not "what you are nor what you have been" that "God looks mercifully upon us, but what you would be."[46]

Dear Lord, hear me when I call upon Your mercy day or night, and may it be always like the dew for my soul as it was for Daniel. As you are merciful to me give me a heart full of tenderness, gentleness and compassion towards others. Amen.

---

44 Farindon, Vol. 1, p. 253.
45 Ibid., pp. 235, 237, 241, 245, 255.
46 *Cloud*, p. 240.

SELF KNOWLEDGE

Wash yourselves; make yourselves clean;
Put away the evil of your doings from before my eyes.

Isaiah 1.16.

Full Readings: Isaiah 1.10, 16-20; Psalm 50. 8-9,16-17, 21, 23; Matthew 23.1-12.

How BEAUTIFUL ARE WE? Today's Gospel is making that challenge. Are we as beautiful on the inside as we show on the outside? As Christians we can never be like the ostrich and hide our heads in the sand. Living out the Christian faith has always involved taking risks, and one of those risks is to discover ourselves with all our moles for that is how God knows us. How sad it is that so many people hide behind some kind of façade or pretend to be another kind of person.

We are also blinded by our own inbuilt prejudices, and intolerances. Yet to be truly our self we have to tap all our doubts, fears and inhibitions which prevent us being the person God has made. He has created each one of us differently and He wants each person to be that unique person as no-one else can do what He wants that person to do and be. He does not want pretence or the perception of another. He wants me to be me, and you to be you. The Jesuit, Anthony de Mello, in a remarkable book suggested that most people go through life asleep and as they have never awakened from their slumber, they have never discovered their real identity.[47]

Lent always provides us with this opportunity, providing we are

---

47 Anthony de Mello, *Awareness* (New York, 1990).

44

willing to seize it, to strip ourselves of all pretence and security and to stand naked before our God. The only security we need in life is the assurance of God's presence, which we have all the time, even when we do not feel His nearness. He has never deserted us, nor is He likely to do so.

You may ask, how can we gain this self-knowledge? How can we honestly discover the real me? Reading the above book undoubtedly would help. A more practical way is through confession. As we kneel in the confessional our souls are truly bared, stripped of any thought of decency almost, and we come to Him as we are with all our sins and scars. There can never be any room for pretence in the confessional, otherwise this sacrament becomes a farce. As Donne expressed it, "there is not a more silly folly, than to think [one can] hide any sinful action from God," while there is "no sounder wisdom than to discover them ... by an humble and penitent confession."[48] We learn as Isaiah teaches us in the first reading today, "though [my] sins be like scarlet, they may become white as snow. Though they be crimson red, they may become white as wool" (Is. 1.18).

By discovering our true selves through examination and confession, we are then able to acknowledge all our prejudices, barriers, pre-conceived ideas, and insecurities as well our true inspiration, hopes and goals. If we are frightened about exposing ourselves to our true selves, ponder on the purpose of our earthly pilgrimage; it is but a preparation for heaven, and in heaven we are what God made us to be. In comparison with what God thinks of us to what others or even myself think is of little consequence. His outstretching arms will always embrace us, while our friends' embraces are sometimes very superficial. Self knowledge allows us to be free and not to worry about other people's opinion or reaction.

During this Lent if we are tempted to wrap ourselves up in cotton wool for whatever reason, learn instead to trust - to trust in Him who loves us so much that He yearns for us to be ourselves. He is our security, our fortress and our rock. There is nothing else we need on this earthly pilgrimage but the surety of His abiding presence, and when we cannot feel His closeness, to trust in His faithfulness. Let go and stretch out your hand to God. I often ponder on that part of Michelangelo's fresco in the Sistine chapel where man's hand reaches

---

48   Donne, *Fifty Sermons*, p. 62.

out to God's outstretched hand. One day they both will meet, never to be separated.

This Lent learn to be your true self, and not be one of the many who go through the motions of living. "We are ... the seed of God", and by growing in godliness and holiness, "we are *partakers of the divine Nature itself*."[49]

Dear God, when I find it difficult to be honest with myself, give me sufficient grace to conquer this, knowing that after this earthly pilgrimage I can only take my true self to heaven. Amen.

---

49   Ibid., p. 51.

Imitatio Christ

Whoever will be chief among you, let him be your servant;
Even as the Son of Man came not to be ministered unto
but to minister, and to give his life a ransom for many.

Matthew 20.27-8.

Full Readings: Jeremiah 18. 8-20; Psalm 31. 5-6, 14–16; Matthew 20. 17-
28.

It took James and John until after the Resurrection to understand what their Lord meant by true discipleship while Jeremiah in the first reading for today certainly knew what it was to suffer for being a prophet in Jerusalem in the pre-exilic period. Later on Paul would also share some of Jeremiah's sufferings as he learnt what it was to be crucified with Christ and to live in Him as expressed in his letter to the Galatians (2.20).

Those who live alone realize it is much easier to live virtuously (although selfishness can become a dangerous sin with all its offshoots) than when we share a house or a place of work with other people. We can only imitate Christ if we are prepared to live with others in this world and following Our Lord's example by withdrawing from it from time to time for spiritual replenishment and renewal.

What exactly do we mean by *imitatio Christi*? It means first of all living as Christ lived while here on earth. In today's Gospel Christ did not rebuke John and James for making their request to sit on either side of Christ in the kingdom through their mother nor the other ten disciples for their consequent anger at the two. Instead He taught them about the nature of His kingdom – whoever wants to be great must learn to be a servant. This involves recognizing every human being as my brother or sister and helping out when it is needed, turning the other cheek when despised or ridiculed, being silent when misunderstood, loving when someone hates and is even physically brutal, and fighting against all kinds of injustices and distortions of the truth. It also means imitating Christ's fasting and praying and above all His obedience. That obedience will make us die with Him in so many ways. So we are called to be Christ-like; in fact He has no other feet or hands to do His work in this world but ours as Teresa once put it.

We also have the example of many saints. Many of the saints of old ardently desired to imitate Christ and felt they could only do this by withdrawing from the world and living alone in the desert, as exemplified by hermits such as Anthony. The saint who came nearest to imitating Christ was St. Francis. One Lent he spent alone on a tiny island in Lake Trasimene, taking with him but two loaves of bread. His intent was to imitate our dear Saviour's fasting and praying in the wilderness for forty days. When he was collected at the end of those forty days he had consumed only half a loaf. This he had eaten out of respect and reverence for his Master. St. Francis willed and lived so much like his beloved Lord that before he died he bore the stigmata of the cross in his body. No wonder he has often been referred to as the second Christ.

Many other saints were like St. Francis in wanting to imitate Christ that they too wanted His passion's imprints on them. Mother Julian in pleading that she may understand His Passion more deeply, desired to suffer "with Him as others did who loved Him", and to feel "all manner of pain, bodily and [spiritual], which I should have had if I ... [had] died."[50] Perhaps we are not called to be another St Francis or Mother Julian, but we are expected to take up our cross daily and follow Him wherever that takes us and whatever it demands.

Imitatio Christi means also asking ourselves in any given situation what would Christ do here? There are many times when we find ourselves in situations when we just do not know what to do. I can remember a few years back one Easter day when my son and I de-

---

50 Julian of Norwich, p.7.

cided to visit his former Music teacher whom neither us had seen for three years or so. When we rang the doorbell a man answered, obviously distressed. I sensed what the situation was, but needless to say I explained that Francis had been a music pupil of his wife, and we had come to visit. With that, the poor man almost broke down, informing us it was exactly twelve months that day since his wife had died. It was clear he wanted to be alone in his grief, but nevertheless he invited us in. Something within me made me say "thank you". However I did not know the next step at all. I prayed vigorously for guidance so that I could leave a little touch of Easter joy with him in his grief. I remember I spoke as if someone within me was speaking very gently and full of love. Soon topics of conversation easily raised themselves as we had a common bond in our love and appreciation of music. I think there were moments that afternoon when he did shelve his grief and he felt a little Easter joy as my son and I ended up staying with him for two hours! Thus in imitating Christ it is as Frank preach, "His way first, and not our own."[51]

During this Lent we have the opportunity to gauge how our lives measure against that of Christ's. If that measure falls short, we have the chance to rectify it. Do remember when we imitate Christ we give a sanctity to our living in this world with all its frailties, faults and foolishness. Don't ever fall into the trap and believe that it is by only escaping this world that we can imitate Christ. We cannot! St. Basil was right when he drew up his community rule! Yet we must also remember that our *imitatio Christi* is only worthwhile if it brings us into a deeper relationship with Christ.

You have taught us dear Lord that we must take up our cross and follow You daily. Fill us with love, tenderness, compassion, patience, tolerance and sensitivity that we may respond to all those who cross our paths each day. Amen.

---

51 Frank, Vol. 1, p. 24.

MEDITATION

Happy are those [whose] … delight is in the
law of the Lord and meditate on it day and night.

Psalm 1.1-2.

Full Readings: Jeremiah 17. 5 - 10; Psalm 1.1- 6; Luke 16. 19-31.

THE ISRAELITES WERE TAUGHT to meditate and study the Torah in order to know how they should live. Indeed as the Psalmist tells us today, this was their delight. In like manner Christians too have been encouraged to read and meditate on Holy Scripture. In the second of the pastoral letters to Timothy, we read that "all Scripture is inspired by God and is useful for teaching, for reproof, for correction, and for training in righteousness" (2 Tim. 3.16). The Bible is one of the principal ways for us to know Christ better. Other ways include the writings of the mystics and saints and sacred icons as well of course of praying.

Earlier on I wrote about stillness. To be able to meditate and concentrate on our reading or visual aid we must have stilled our souls and blocked out all extraneous noise. It is imperative that we have silence around and within us. Silence is sometimes like an oasis in the desert in this modern world, hard to find, but when it is, how refreshing. We must find it and make room for it in our lives, especially for meditation. Rather than seeing silence as strength, some of us are frightened of it, as if we are left naked without it. The irony of this, is that we need both for meditation, silence to listen to what we read, and nakedness to let what we hear penetrate into our souls.

50

What is the best time for meditation? The most important thing is to have a set time each day. Some will find it best early in the morning, some after breakfast, while some before dinner and so on. However I do urge you not to plan to do it at that time of the day when you are most fatigued. Tiredness and meditation usually do not go together; it becomes more like a dreaming exercise! Thus for meditation to be constructive we do need to be alert.

Most people who meditate regularly have a set plan for it. Some use the lessons for Mass or the Offices for each day, while others have what are called Bible Study booklets, and some may use the devotional writings of the saints. Those of us who adhere to the Catholic faith tend to have their readings revolving around daily readings at Mass and the keeping of the feasts and fasts of the Christian year. Whichever way we choose for our meditation, the first thing we have to do is to pray for the guidance of the Holy Spirit to enlighten and inspire us. Once we have read the passage we try to visualize it and in a sense live it out by placing ourselves in the context. After that we often find ourselves focusing on some aspect more than the rest. It may be simply a word or a phrase which sparks off our thinking. This usually brings a response either in relation to our own life with God or leads us to dwell on some attribute of Him. Usually our meditation finishes with making some kind of resolution. Thus for instance during Holy Week our focal point in our readings will make us respond to some aspects of Christ's passion and crucifixion. Whatever we meditate upon, it brings a certain intensity which in turn brings a reality. If we meditate, for example, long enough on aspects of the passion, we do end up sharing in a small way something of the suffering of our dear Saviour, and feel remorse for our part in causing such pain to Him. That is of course the whole purpose of meditation. Taylor explained:

> The use of meditation is to consider any of the mysteries of religion with purposes to draw from its rules of life, or affections of virtue or detestation of voice; and from hence the man rises to devotion, and mental prayer and intercourse with God; and after that He rests himself in the bosom of beatitude and is swallowed up with the comprehension of love and contemplation.

He also stressed that the fruits of our meditation must be seen in living the "good life".[52]

Our meditations enable us to move onto the next step in the spiritual life, contemplation - a subject for another day.

One other thought as well as meditating at our regular time each day, there are usually some other times during the day when we can semi-meditate. If alone at meal times, a devotional book makes a good companion as it does when travelling. Invariably there are always those times when we have to sit and wait. Wait, by waiting upon the Lord. There are many books on various aspects of spirituality that make good meditative material, and help us to live in communion with God. Be a meditative Christian this Lent.

Dear God may I through my regular times of meditation, so read, mark and inwardly digest the Scriptures that I may come "to know You more clearly, love You more dearly and follow You more nearly day by day. Amen."[53]

---

52   Taylor, Vol. 2, pp. 135, 143.
53   This is part of the Prayer of St. Richard of Chichester.

JUDGMENT

*'I say unto you, The kingdom of God will be taken from
you and given to a nation bringing forth the fruits thereof.'*
Matthew 21. 43.

Full Readings: Genesis 37.3-4, 12-13, 17-28; Psalm 105. 16 – 21; Matthew
21. 33 – 46.

CHRIST MADE IT CLEAR that our lives are being constantly judged by
His teaching as evident in the parable of the vineyard, today's Gospel
reading. It is a little frightening at times to know this but at the same
times sobering. The best example in the Gospels for Christ's teaching on this is in one of the signs in John's Gospel, the healing of the
man blind from birth in chapter nine. Jesus approached a man who
has been blind from birth and has never known light, only a world
of darkness; so he has never experienced the wonder and beauty of
God in nature. He represents each one of us, as we are all born blind
through original sin, until our eyes are opened by Him who takes
away the sin of the world. In this healing, Our Lord's act is both creative and sacramental. He makes clay, a creative act to give light from
darkness, whereby He is re-enacting that first act of the Trinitarian
God in creating light out of darkness (Gen. 1.3). It is also sacramental
as this visible sign leads to healing grace. Christ anointed the blind
man's eyes with this clay, just as the catechumen is exorcized before
baptism, and sent him to wash in the pool of Siloam, just as the catechumen is led to the baptismal waters. John deliberately informed
us that the meaning of Siloam is "Sent". The man is sent; he went

without hesitation, the same as Christ did when He came to earth when sent by the Father. "Lo I come to do your will, O God." And "Fit me a Body, for I resolve to be made Flesh" (Heb. 10.5,7). After washing as commanded, the man found that he no longer lived in darkness - he could see, He was a new person, just as the washing in baptism makes the catechumen a new person, the child of God and a member of Christ, and an inheritor of the kingdom of God.

The former blind man's enlightenment is juxtaposed against the refusal of the Pharisees to hear Christ's words, thus revealing their preference to live in darkness rather than the light as this would have exposed their sins. At the end of this whole episode, Christ declared, "It is for judgment that I came into this world - to give sight to the sightless and to make blind those who see" (Jn 9.39). That Light enables us to see our deeds, know our thoughts and perceive right from wrong, and so we are consequently being judged by it.

The Gospel for today also reminds us that we face a general judgment, what is sometimes referred to as Judgment Day when we render an account of our lives. Just as we cannot escape death in this life, so we cannot escape judgment. "'We shall all stand before the judgment-seat of Christ.' None of us must think to escape. There we must give [an] account [for] what we have done amiss; every action, every idle word, every vain and wanton thought, every inward desire, must we yield account of it in the day of judgment," preached Frank during Advent.[54] The Gospel assures us that Our Lord will be our judge. In this we can derive much comfort because we shall have as our Judge One who knows what it is to be man and to know all our temptations, trials and tribulations as He shared all our experiences except sin.

Thus on Judgment Day we shall be judged according to how we have lived. Although God is all love and mercy, He is also just. He will go to infinite pains to save our souls, but ultimately if we continue to live in sin and ignore all His pleadings, then we have to face the consequences. In a sense it is the way we live in either responding to or ignoring God's love and mercy and reciprocating that with others that works as our judge.

This is obvious from the Gospel that on Judgment Day we shall also be judged on our good works. It is not enough to believe and

---

54 Frank, Vol. 1. p. 37.

be pious in our daily living. We cannot turn a deaf ear or a blind eye to the needs of our brothers and sisters. We must learn to give selflessly to others, that is, be put out in some way to meet their needs. Everybody can give when it does not hurt in regards to time, wealth or goods. But that is not the giving our Lord is speaking of when He bids us to feed the hungry, give drink to the thirsty, to lodge the stranger, to clothe the poor and to visit the prisoner and sick. By rendering these loving acts we are doing them to Him, and when we neglect them we are failing to do them to Christ. Do we want to hear Him say to us, "Depart from me, you cursed into everlasting fire" (Mt. 25. 41) on Judgment day?

In performing these works of mercy we must also have our motivation rightly channelled as we must never do them as kind of blackmail to secure heaven rather than hell. God knows our hearts and so good works like our praying must be always undertaken with a pure intent. It can be another form of selfishness to do charitable work simply to save our own soul. One of my very favourite prayers is this one by St. Francis Xavier that has become a well-known hymn.

> Then why, O blessèd Jesus Christ,
> 　　　Should I not love thee well?
> Not for the sake of winning heaven,
> 　　　Nor of escaping hell.
>
> Not with hope of gaining aught,
> 　　　Not seeking a reward,
> But as thyself has lovèd me,
> 　　　O ever loving Lord. ...
>
> E'en so I love thee, and will love,
> 　　　And in thy praises will I sing,
> Solely because thou art my God
> 　　　And my eternal King.[55]

When will Judgment Day happen? The Caroline Divine, Mark Frank in one of his Advent sermons explains this.

Yet when this 'then' will be, when that day and hour will come,

---

55　*New English Hymnal*, p. 114.

'no man knows, no, not the Son of man' Himself, as man; He who could tell you that come He would, and could tell you the immediate signs that would forerun it, knew not then the time when those signs should be, or knew it not to tell you; that we might always be waiting for His coming.

Had it been fit for us to know, no doubt He would have told us; but so far unnecessary it seems to be acquainted with that secret time, that He gives us signs which rather puzzle than instruct us; signs which we sometimes think fulfilled already; signs which have often been the forerunners of particular ruins and fates of countries and kingdoms; signs which at the same time we fear past already, yet think they are not; that so by this hard dialect of tokens in heaven and earth, we might behold our presumptuous curiosity deluded into a perpetual watching for this last coming. ...

It is enough for us to know there will be a day of judgment, against which we must provide every day to make up our accounts, lest that day come upon us unawares, lest death at least hurry us away to our particular doom, which will there leave us, where the last judgment will be sure to find us, in the same condition; no power or tears of ours being then able to change or alter it.[56]

During this Lent let us examine how we live in the light of knowing we meet the Son of man as our Judge on that last day.

O Holy Spirit, inspire me with good deeds and thoughts to meet the needs of others in my daily life. Give me grace also to persevere unto the end, and to know through the example of Lot's wife I must serve You faithfully until I die. Amen.

---

56 Frank, Vol. 1, p. 36.

THANKSGIVING

Bless the Lord, O my soul:
And all that is within me,
bless his holy name.

Psalm 103.1.

Full Readings: Micah 7.14-5; 18-20, Psalm 103. 1-4, 9-12; Luke 15.1-3, 11-32.

OUR OPENING PRAYER EACH morning should be one of thanksgiving for a new day and for rest during the night in order to arise in good spirits. I often say if we can put our feet on the floor each morning we indeed have much for which to thank God, as is expressed in the opening of the set Psalm for today. Many of our ejaculatory prayers are ones of thanksgiving. Some of these from the Psalter are "I will give thanks unto You, O Lord, with my whole heart" (Ps. 9.1), "Unto You, O God, do we give thanks; yes, unto You do we give thanks (Ps.75.1) and "O give thank unto the Lord, for He is gracious: and His mercy endures for ever" (Ps.136.1).

For those who still hanker after the language of the Book of Common Prayer, one of the loveliest of its prayers is the General Thanksgiving. What a shame its sentiments are not heard more often in our churches to-day as it sums up all those loving acts and mercies God has done, and is doing for us. However even if is not said very often publicly, that does not mean we cannot use it in our devotional prayers or at least use it as a model. In this thanksgiving we offer up our heartfelt thanks for what God as the Father has given us, namely our creation, daily preservation and His mercy; as the Son in redeeming us and giving us "the hope of glory"; and as the Holy Spirit who bestows His grace upon us, and thus gives us the potential to holiness of living.

If we do not already do it, let God share in all those happy and unexpected pleasures and delightful moments we have from time to time, often so spontaneously. Furthermore just as we should examine our conscience at the end of each day for the sins we have committed against God, others and self, so we also should make the habit of thanking Him, not collectively, but actually singling out everything for which we have caused to be grateful on that day. On the surface we may think there is not anything for which to say thank you. After all it has been one of those days when everything has seemed to go wrong. Yet if we dig deep, and a little deeper there is always something for which we can express our thanks, even if it is the mere feat of surviving the day! Just as it is true that we should not let the sun go down upon our wrath, so it should not upon our ungratefulness, as the prodigal son eventually learnt. Mother Julian reminds us that "thanksgiving is a true inward knowing, with great reverence and lowly dread, turning ourself with all our might unto the working that our Lord stirs us to rejoicing and thanking inwardly." She continued, "Truly to rejoice in our Lord is a full, lovely, thanking in his sight."[57]

By making thanksgiving a focal point of praying each day, it means we shall never take anything for granted. Kronstadt reminds us, "Thank God every day with your whole heart for having given to you life according to His image and likeness." When we do this, "prayer is a state of continual gratitude."[58] Our thanksgiving to God will spill over in our giving thanks to others in our daily living too. Even the smallest things done for us should be acknowledged. Our genuine thanks not only help us towards growing in humility but also in recognizing the worth of others.

If we are truly thankful for our blessings in life, it should make us more conscious and concerned for those who live in perpetual poverty and hunger and cold. True thanksgiving means we do something to help our brothers and sisters throughout the world who have less than us.

---

57 Julian of Norwich, p. 135.
58 Kronstadt, *Counsel*, p. 13.

Lent is a good time to recall those sobering words of our Lord, "Inasmuch as you did it not to one of the least of these, you did it not to me" (Mt. 25.45). Hopefully our thanksgiving will make us more susceptible to the needs of others and prompt us to respond.

Heavenly Father, You have blessed me abundantly in this life. Help me to show my thankfulness in the way I live "by giving up [myself] to Your service, and by walking before You in holiness and righteousness all [my] days." Amen.[59]

---

59 An extract from the Prayer of Thanksgiving from the Book of Common Prayer.

THE THIRD SUNDAY IN LENT

FAITHFULNESS

So when the Samaritans were come unto Jesus,
they besought him that he would tarry:
and he abode there two days.
And many more believed because of his own word.

John 4. 40-1.

Full Readings:

Cycle A: Exodus 17.3-7; Psalm 95; Romans 5.1-2, 5-8; John 4. 5-42.

Cycle B: Exodus 20.1-17; Psalm 18; 1 Corinthians 1.22-25; John 2.13.

Cycle C: Exodus 3.1-8, 13-15; Psalm 102; 1 Corinthians 10.1-6, 10-12; Luke 13.1-9.

THE CYCLE A READINGS are compulsory in parishes preparing cate-chumens for baptism at the Paschal Vigil. The Gospel unfolds the meeting Christ had firstly with a Samaritan woman at the well of Jacob near Sychar, and secondly with Samaritans in her village. After our Lord had spoken with the woman she acknowledged that He is indeed the promised Messiah and ran back into her village to tell others that she has found the Messiah. They in turn invited Jesus to teach them too and came to recognize Him as "the Saviour of the world" (v. 42). These Samaritans set an example of faithfulness to us, especially for those undergoing the first scrutiny.

When baptized we promise or the promise was made on our be-half to "continue Christ's faithful soldier and servant unto our lives' end." This means we have to be faithful to His commandments, and accept His teaching as the truth and the basis for how we live. Thus

60

we cannot pick and choose what areas we shall be faithful to Christ. When Jesus told us to leave our gift at the altar and first be reconciled with the brother/sister we have injured, He meant for us to do that. When He told us to love one another, He meant that too. When He told us "to do this in remembrance of Me", He meant the Eucharist to be celebrated. There are no buts in faithfulness. It is total surrender to His will and bowing to His love and going wherever that takes us. So faithfulness demands obedience, and demands it now. To the would-be disciple who wanted to bury his father first, Our Lord told Him, to "let the dead bury their dead" (Lk. 9.60).

Christ asks us take up our cross daily and to follow Him. If we are trying to live the Christian life, there are all kinds of situation we meet that encroach upon our faithfulness. For example: television viewing challenges the time for meditation and prayer; the cashier's mistake in our favour challenges our honesty; going to the beach or shopping on Sunday challenges our attendance at the Eucharist; listening to smutty jokes challenges our purity; over-eating at the dining table challenges our temperance; and listening to gossip challenges our love for our neighbour. As Christians we are, for example, called to point out that smutty jokes degrade the dignity of man, and our first priority on Sunday, except in rare cases, is the Eucharist. Unfortunately so many of us act very timidly in these and likeminded situations. We are more concerned with what people think of us as we shun disapproval. If this is our response most of the time, we have not started to take up the cross. What is important is to witness to His truth and justice in this world. If that makes us unpopular and misunderstood, it is not all that important, because it is only what God thinks of us that matters. We may think it is all right to turn a blind eye to the cashier's mistake, but God does not turn a blind eye to us.

Faithfulness means integrity in every situation. Thus there are many times when we have to choose what we know God wants us to be and to do, and what the world, friends and relations are demanding of us. Better for us to feel the shame of the world now, than later to experience God's rebuff. Remember having put our hands to the plough, there is no turning back. Otherwise we make ourselves unfit for His kingdom.

Christ wants our faithfulness. "Who is not with Me, is against Me." It is very clear cut. To those who find it hard to be loyal to Him where we work, within our family or friends, ask yourself, "How faithful am I in my prayer life and receiving Him in the Sacrament?" If we can be faithful to Him in prayer and sacrament, we shall find it easier to be His faithful servant in our everyday situations too. As we grow in our love for Him, we become fearless for Christ's sake.

Being faithful in our prayer time means that we not only pray when it is convenient for us or when we feel like it but also deliberately give time to God, even though we think we have one hundred and one things to do. Those things will always be there, but time to save our souls is even more precious. This can never be put off, and is at the heart of our overall faithfulness to Christ and our growth in holiness.

There is also our faithfulness to our spouse, families and friends. Sirach tells us "A faithful friend is the medicine of life; and they that fear the Lord shall find him" (Sir. 6.16). Friendship is one of the treasures of life and thrives on faithfulness. Even at His betrayal Jesus referred to Judas as "friend" (Mt. 26.49) though he had forfeited faithfulness to his Master. In the ancient Roman world, *amicitia* was extremely valued and was the basis for the code of conduct. Hence the relation of a friend to a friend was regarded in the same light of that between brothers. This modern world could learn from this about the ethics of conduct.

Use Lent as a time to start being faithful in little things to Christ and to others and it will be like throwing a stone in a pool.

Dear Lord through your Spirit help me to be faithful to You in both little and big things in life and thus imitate Your faithfulness to Your Father. Amen.

SUFFERING

*And all those in the synagogue when they heard
these things, were filled with wrath,
And they rose up, and thrust Jesus out of the city,
and led him unto the brow of the hill whereon
their city was built, … [to]cast him down headlong.*

Luke 4. 28-9.

Full Readings: 2 Kings 5.1-15; Psalm 42. 2-3, 43. 3-4; Luke 4. 24-30.

SUFFERING COMES IN MANY ways. For Christ, some of His sufferings were through misunderstanding of His word as recorded in today's Gospel, while Naaman suffered from leprosy that could have forced him to be an outcast. However after being prompted by his servants he followed the command of Elisha and washed himself seven times in the Jordan for healing.

Christ also taught us that to follow Him involves the cross. Thus there are many ways in which we suffer for Christ even when we are not like the saints who openly welcomed and embraced suffering to be more Christ-like. Yet our faithfulness to our Saviour will often cause much pain and grief. Those of us who try to live Christ-like in a family or work situation which are not Christian know this. Apart from the sadness we feel because these people are not living in the fullest sense, there are the times when we are ridiculed, misunderstood, and provoked because we insist on living according to Christ's standard and not the shady ones of this world.

What heart ache is felt by the teenager who arises early on Sunday morning to go to Mass and has abuse hurled at him/her as he/she opens the door to leave. Or the wife who has waited hours for her husband to return from the pub for his evening meal, only to be greeted with, "I don't want any", and then the next morning is shouted at for going to her parish church instead of getting his breakfast. Or in the office when we politely point out it is stealing to take office equipment for our own use, we are told "it's not our concern." Yet we know it is! Or the anguish suffered by a woman when her husband continually criticizes her for her time spent in prayer, and does not care how often he interrupts. Or the Mother who has tried to bring up her son as a Christian and is told when he reaches his adult years, "It is all rubbish, this loving God and loving your neighbour, and if you are such a fool to believe in such things look at the atrocities committed daily throughout the world." There are still many St. Monica's in the world!

Whenever I think of Christians being persecuted by their families I always think of Sadhu Sundar Singh. Whatever our sufferings have been, it is nothing compared to his sufferings when he was ostracised by his Sikh family when he became a Christian in the early twentieth century. Rejected by both family and society he became an outcast and spent the rest of his life preaching the Gospel. He became one of the great mystics of the twentieth century. You can learn more about him in his book *At the Master's Feet*.

There is also the suffering from actual physical pain because of illness and long termed sicknesses. How do we reconcile such suffering with a loving God? Why do we have to suffer? What have I done to deserve all this? These are questions which are asked over and over again and there is no miracle answer to them. We do know as Sadu Singh put it that "the laws of God are intended for the spiritual health and happiness of man" but if we oppose them this "brings about spiritual pain and suffering." If you have ever suffered excruciating pain, you know it is very difficult to concentrate on much else, even praying. As I said previously this is a situation where the Jesu prayer is most effective. That one word over and over again lets us hold on. The other strength comes from knowing that as we suffer pain, intense pain, agonizing pain, that at last we have a taste of our Lord's physical suffering. It is the Cross which makes sense of all sufferings: physical, mental and spiritual. Singh called the Cross as the key to heaven while Mother Julian pointed out that Christ's love was so strong that He deliberately and ardently chose to suffer for us. Indeed "He suffered more pain than all men of salvation, that ever were from the first beginning unto the last day" could experience or imagine."[60]

Furthermore there is the suffering of our souls when in prayer we feel desolate and devoid of any spiritual comfort. Everything is parched and barren, like being in a desert and never reaching the oasis for replenishment. Not only does God seem to have abandoned us, but we also struggle in our stretching out to Him. This is what St. John of the Cross calls "the dark night of the soul". We can also identify with Jeremiah when he cried out, "Surely against me is He turned; ... He has built against me, and compassed me with gall and travail. He has set me in dark places, ... He has hedged me about, that I cannot get out: He has made my chain heavy" (Lam. 3.2,4-5). Of all suffering this is probably the hardest to endure for Christians sincerely seeking to live with Christ. I shall write at more length on darkness on another day.

One other point about our suffering - the more we suffer, the more we can identify with others. Until we have been there, we do not know what it is really like, no matter how much we empathize. Thus suffering usually brings with it a sincere compassion and patience with others. It also enables us to sort out what really is important in life and what is not. Suffering, whatever kind, can also be the mean for growth and strengthening. If seen in this light we can endure all for Him Who endured all for us.

Dear Lord, You did not despise the shame and the suffering of the cross. Grant me the strength to suffer joyfully any pain, darkness, affliction, ridicule and abuse for You. Let it be a time of growing in loving service to You and others. Amen.

---

60 Singh, p. 60; Julian of Norwich, p. 69.

Forgiveness

'Lord, how often must shall my brother
sin against me, and forgive him?

Matthew 18. 21.

Full Readings: Daniel 3. 25, 34-43; Psalm 25.4-9; Matthew 18.21-35.

PETER WAS UNDOUBTEDLY SURPRISED by Christ's answer to his question, not only seven times must he forgive but also seventy times seven. That means always. Whenever we say the Lord's Prayer, which for many Christians is quite a few times daily, we ask God to forgive us our sins, but we must forgive others for it to be granted. Luke spelt this out very simply: "Forgive, and you will be forgiven" (Lk. 6.37). One of the barriers to loving others is that we have never been able to forgive them for what they are, or for what wrong we feel they have done to us. Put another way we cannot really love unless we do forgive.

It is no accident that forgiveness has been described as the heart of the Gospel, and the backbone of being a Christian. In the Orthodox Church, the Sunday before Lent is called *the Sunday of Forgiveness*. This surely emphasizes that before we seek forgiveness for our sins we need to mend our broken relationships with whom we live and work. This involves not only forgiving others but seeking forgiveness from them for our sins against them. Christ died for all of us and so all mankind shares in His act of forgiveness.

In one of his loveliest Pentecost sermons, Andrewes described God's forgiveness as His breath breathing forgiveness upon penitents and dispelling sin that is like "a mist or fog, that men are lost in," and blown away by His breath. He elaborated. It was a breath, a "pestilent breath of the serpent, that blew upon our first parents, infected [and] poisoned them at the first." Now at Pentecost, "Christ's breath" enters and "cures it - breath by breath." From "the breath of His mouth virtue goes from it," and before it "sin cannot stand" as it is blown "away like a little dust."[61]

To those who say, "I can forgive, but not forget", I say it is not true. Once we truly forgive, we forget the hurt (that does not mean we forget the incident but we no longer attach any anger or revenge to it) because we have let that bundle go, and laid it at the foot of the cross. If we find ourselves still carrying the hurt, then we have not truly forgiven. There is no point in asking for forgiveness for ourselves unless we are prepared to forgive others. "If thy heart tells thee that thou forgivest thy brother, doubt not but God does likewise forgive thee," preached Andrewes.

However if we find it difficult to forgive another person, one sobering thought should be that I too am a sinner. Is my brother's sin any worse than mine? Is the speck in my brother's eye any worse than the beam in my eye? We know that our Lord through His own temptations in the desert is more compassionate towards us. In like manner "we ... having been tempted ourselves, ... [should] look upon others' defects with a more passionate regard" and imitate our Lord's compassion.[62] That is why using the sacrament of Confession/Reconciliation regularly is healthy as well as a spiritual exercise as it enables us to see ourselves as God sees us and sometimes it is not very nice, and perhaps no nicer than the person we rub shoulders with at work and judge. By acknowledging that, we should be more kindly disposed towards others.

As Donne tells us, one of the most assuring aspects of being a Christian is to know that God is always more than ready to forgive our "relapses into sins repented, ... faint repentances, ... sinful thoughts, ... blasphemous words ... [and] sins against [our] neighbour, ... and self."[63]

If He is ready to forgive us over and over again, we too must be prepared to forgive quickly and often. Nevertheless as part of the

---

61 Andrewes, Vol. 3, pp. 266, 268.
62 Ibid.,Vol. 5, pp. 436, 486.
63 Donne *Eighty Sermons*, p. 343.

forgiving process we are sometimes called to explain the wrongness of the sin of our brethren. When doing this it must be done under the shadow of the Holy Spirit in a very caring manner, devoid of any judgmental approach, to show that sin fragments any relationship with God, and we jeopardize our growth in holiness by pursuing that sin.

This Lent as we examine our consciences, if we find any hidden grudges there, confront them and not bury them. We cannot live the Christian life unless we live in the spirit of repentance and forgiveness. Be a forgiving person this Lent.

My dear Saviour, grant me a forgiving heart to everyone so I can always seek Your forgiveness when I sin. Amen.

TIME

Think not I have come to destroy the law or the prophets.
Matthew 5.17.

Full Readings: Deuteronomy 4.1, 5-9; Psalm 148.12-20; Matthew 5.17-19.

THE ISRAELITES, AS TODAY'S readings illustrate, were expected to keep the commandments so that all could live harmoniously. Amongst those laws were those for caring for family and neighbour as reflected in the second great commandment. Caring for people involves time – our topic for today. Next to our love, time is the most precious gift we can give to God, family and neighbour. Yet we jealously guard it, almost like life itself. However it must be spent lavishly on God and others. St. Bernard tells us "Time is only that we may find God." We are given a life time for this, but how much of our time do we give Him? Is it very much? And how much time do we set aside especially to be with Him in prayer? When we do, is it a good selection of time when we are alert and able to concentrate? Or do we give God the leftovers? That is, when we've done all we have wanted for the day, He can have what is left when we are too tired to do anything else anyway.

Christ gave us the example of how we should distribute time. He gave a considerable proportion of it in prayer, an example we should follow. The time we spend with God in prayer and stillness should be like offering an unblemished lamb; it is the best; it is not something that is crammed in between various activities. It also should be like the breaking of day and therefore the freshest. That is why there is a lot to be said for making early morning the main praying time of the day. If you have never given God the best time yet, now this Lent is the time. It may mean getting up earlier, which in turn might mean going to bed earlier. It is all a matter of having our priorities in the right order. Once having that, then our time with God in prayer, meditation and contemplation becomes the most precious use of time for the day.

Time given to others is almost as important. Although we may have set time aside for God in our prayer life, very few of us see that we have to serve God all day. This invariably means that when we are in a hurry to get to work in the morning, we shove or growl at anyone in our way, rather than our standing aside to let the other person through. Or, if the front door bell goes, when we are about to leave, we usually mutter something like "damn", and be almost impolite as we open the door. We don't give the person a chance to be heard because we are too pre-occupied with the thought, "I'll have to rush now". When we arrange to entertain in our home, it usually is to suit us and to fit in with our routine, and then we don't expect our guests to stay too late! But how often are we late for appointments and inconvenience others through our own selfish use of time?

When was the last time that you gave time to visit someone in need, someone in loneliness, someone in pain who longs to have another person's company to break up the monotony of getting through a day? When was the last time you dropped doing what you were working on in order to meet the need of a fellow human being? When was the last time you wrote a letter to a friend or picked up the 'phone to talk to a lonely person? Time is either spent selfishly or selflessly. There is no *via media*. Time is not my gift but God's. We have no doubt heard many times that "Time is made for man, and not man for time." Let us heed it in our relationships with our brothers and sisters.

This Lent we also need to ask more specifically when was the last time we spent time at home with our families? A marriage to work effectively means giving time to each other so interests and concerns can be shared. Parents need to give time to be with their children, and to listen to them and share thoughts and experiences with them. Pray with them, laugh with them, cry with them, play with them and read to them. It all involves time, but remember it is the most precious thing you can give to a child next to love. As we grow older we shall look upon those moments as being very precious times in our lives.

Most of us are very good at wasting time. Lent is a time to ask ourselves, "How much time do I actually waste?" By that I don't mean when things go wrong as that can be a growing time, but when we squander time by pursuing nothingness. How much time do we spend on purely selfish endeavours which have no overtones for others? For instance how many of us spend a great part of our time in simply day-dreaming? Obviously each person must have some time to him/herself each week. We all need living space. However when we over indulge in time spent on self, then it becomes sinful.

Most of us are also good at not savouring and enjoying now, the present moment in time. So often we want to live in the future by forgetting the present, and so we use this for planning for the future such as what we shall do when we are finished the present task or of more exotic thoughts of what we shall do when we retire. We have to learn to live in the sacrament of the moment. To-morrow may never come on this earth.

Sometimes too we spend our time from day to day in a very unrealistic way, as if we were only making a draft of living in preparation for a better life which will be begin someday, but not now. How foolish this approach is, because that someday never comes!

Ultimately we are given time in this life to prepare us for the time when time is timeless, and when our whole existence is outside of time. Lent gives us the opportunity to see how that preparation is going. How we spend our time here on earth determines whether we are summoned to heaven or hell. There is much truth in the truism "We are living on borrowed time!"

Dear God teach me to see time as very precious. Let me never be guilty of squandering it all on myself but to see it as a gift to spend on others and prepare for my meeting with You on Judgment day. Amen.

THURSDAY AFTER THE THIRD SUNDAY IN LENT

LISTENING

So you shall speak all these words unto them:
but they will not hearken to you.

Jeremiah 7. 27.

Full Readings: Jeremiah 7. 23-28; Psalm 95. 1-2, 6-9; Luke 11.14 -23.

THE FIRST READING TELLS of how deaf the Israelites were to Jeremiah's message about God's judgment upon them for their evil ways. They not only did not listen to him on this occasion but also continued to ignore the warnings from this prophet who proclaimed frequently that if they did not repent Jerusalem would lay in ruins, and they would be deported to a strange land.

Very little has changed since the time of Jeremiah. We still don't listen, either to others or even to nature very well. When I lived in Oxford one of the loveliest aspects of my early morning run along the banks of the Cherwell was to listen to the song and smell the scent of nature as it awakened and greeted the new day. Sometimes I would sit on top of a style before jumping over simply to take in the different sounds and to be stunned by the harmony of song. It is a stimulus for the day! How much so was evident when I juxtaposed all this sweetness to the throbbing of engines as I crossed a busy main road to return home.

Thus one of the reasons for poor listening to-day is because of noise. It has intruded and penetrated itself into our lives so that we are bombarded with it continuously. Some of these noises are extraneous and out of our control, but many others are self imposed. For instance, often the first thing in the morning is to turn on the radio or television not softly, but loudly and intrusively. To a certain extent this background noise has taken the place of people. Worse still is the domination of television in the evenings which takes precedence over family conversation around the dinner table. Alas, the screen has devoured conversation. We do not give ourselves a chance to listen to each other and to share our daily experiences, joys, achievements and even our failures and upsets. Unfortunately the art of conversation is being lost.

Apart from the noise level deafening our ears, there are other reasons, probably more serious, for not listening. We do not listen to others and life because basically we do not want to. Listening means forgetting ourselves, and more particularly what we want to say; it means giving our undivided attention to another person, and alas many cannot do that. Some people are so bad at listening that they don't even wait until a person has finished speaking before they interrupt. Many television programmes set poor standards and examples of this. It is also very disturbing when one goes to a meeting and finds someone pursuing the same argument all night, simply because he/she has not bothered to listen to what is being said! What makes us think what we want to say is more important anyway? It only becomes important when it contributes to the point of debate.

It is no wonder that relationships are breaking down, even alas within marriages. When we do not listen to what the other is saying, communications fail and before long, in the case of a husband and wife, each is living a separate life. The same applies to the family. How distressing it is to hear a parent say to a child, "I have not time to listen to you now." But the now is perpetual! Somehow some parents think by giving children everything they want materially compensates for not being a proper parent which means being available to listen time and time again. After all "a word can do more than a gift, and a kind word counts for more than a rich present" (Sir.18:16-7).

However for Christians it should be otherwise. When we realize we have no life but in our neighbour, we accept that as Christians we must be open to one another. No man is an island, and we basically need one another for true growth in Christ. The whole purpose of the shedding of the Spirit at Pentecost was to reconnect each of us with the other. So when another person speaks to us we have to be prepared to listen. This means giving full attention to the person speaking. By concentrating we begin to identify and from this grows involvement in what the other person is trying to communicate so that we can respond in a meaningful way. Listening takes energy and patience and above all love. It often means exposing ourselves to vulnerability and risks as we respond, but that is what the Christian faith is all about.

Listening can act as a good therapy for others too. There are so many souls desperately crying out for someone to listen to them. I am reminded of this constantly when travelling or having coffee. I recall one time I sat opposite an elderly lady in a café before seeing a play, and as I sat she said, "I am just having a little rest before going", and then the flood gates opened. The book I was carrying stayed in my bag. For her to talk and share company for a few minutes with another human being was a means to unleash her loneliness and some of her problems. I don't how many times she said, "I better be off", and five minutes on she was still there. It may not always be convenient to stop and chat, but living out the Gospel is never convenient. We are needed to reach out to such people wherever we find them in life and to be prepared to listen to them and hear what they are saying to us.

If our day is always filled with discordant sounds, and we are only hearing ourselves, then it is little wonder that the still small voice of God has not had a chance to penetrate into our lives. Yet if we want to be good listeners to our neighbour or child, it means we first have to listen to God. We have to learn there are such things as silence and stillness in life in order to give God a sporting chance to speak to us. We don't give Him that when we are continually exposing ourselves to noise. We have to be like the young Samuel, ready and anxious to hear the Lord. He wanted to know God's will for him, and so he waited in the quietness of the night (1 Sam.3.9). We too can discover God's will for us by learning to listen to Him during our prayer time each day. Lent is a time to start, if we have not already done so to listen to God and others.

Dear Lord, You have taught me that I must be a neighbour to all, so help me to be a good listener. Amen.

FRIDAY AFTER THE THIRD SUNDAY IN LENT

PEACE

For the ways of the Lord are right
and the just shall walk in them:
but the transgressors shall fall therein.

Hosea 14. 9.

Full Readings: Hosea 14.2-10; Psalm 81. 6-11, 14, 17; Mark 12. 28 – 34.

THE PROPHETS, INCLUDING HOSEA constantly reminded the Israelites they could live peacefully by repenting of their sins. Likewise if our being is in turmoil all the time we shall never discover the kingdom of God. Ideally we can only live in peace if we are at one with God, that is, living in a state of grace. We too have to respond to Hosea's message and recognize the importance of repentance and confession in our lives so we can leave in peace. It is only penitents who can truly know the peace which Our Lord came to bring to us.

Once we have tasted this peace, nothing will or should shake us from it. That peace of mind enables us to face all kinds of problems and difficulties in life without worrying unduly about them. Yet worrying and anxiety seem to be part of modern living. If we find ourselves spending too much time worrying about problems and other aspects of our lives then we have not learnt to trust in Christ who provides for all, just as He feeds "the birds of the air". Heed His words. He is the only prop we need on our pilgrimage.

We need peace within to pray effectively. "Prayer is the issue of a quiet mind, of untroubled thoughts," stated Taylor. Come to prayer in calmness and discover that "prayer is the peace of our spirit, the stillness of our thoughts, the evenness of recollection, the rest of our cares, and the calm of our tempest."[64]

Peace can never be achieved by worldly comforts as the "soul is still tortured on the rank of restless discontents and self-vexation," suggested Sydenham. It is only when the soul "fastens upon an object infinite both in endlessness and perfection," can the soul be admitted "to the face of God by beatific vision," and experience the "pleasure, and fullness of joy flowing thence." Here the soul "expires in the bosom of God, and lies down softly with sweetest peace and full contentment in the embracement of everlasting bliss."[65]

Another Caroline Divine, Anthony Farindon believed that "a quiet mind of untroubled thoughts" was "a conditional gift" from God in order that the Christian may in turn give to others. Therefore this inward peace must lead us to carry out the work of the Gospel, as it "spreads itself over the poor, and relieves them, over the malicious and melts them, over the injurious man and forgives him, over the violent man, and overcomes him by standing the shock."[66]

At the Eucharist one of the focal points is the *pax* when we exchange with those nearest to us a sign of peace that conveys our peace towards them as well as Christ's. Like St. Francis we are called to be instruments of peace where there is any disharmony. "Those who live by the sword will perish by sword." Otherwise the *pax* during the Mass has no significance.

In exchanging the peace of Christ what in fact are we declaring - that same peace that Jesus talked about at the Last Supper table and manifested during His passion. He thus demands us to pursue peace in a similar way. Therefore in His kingdom there is no place for violence or terrorizing or war but peace only. Very often this means having to turn the other cheek, and absorb the hurt we suffer. But that is the only way to overcome all violence. If we don't absorb it, who will? Retaliation is contrary to Christ's teaching as illustrated in His last twenty-four hours. He did not lift a hand, He did not strike back, He did not utter a simple rebuke but absorbed it all, even though it meant death, death on a cross. He demands the same of us, if we are truly His followers.

Peace is the only answer to all the evils in this world. Violence

---

64 Taylor, Vol. 4, p. 61.
65 Sydenham, pp. 33 - 4.
66 Farindon, Vol. 1, pp. 317, 324.

meeting violence of any kind is a negative action and never achieves anything but causes more violence and destruction as we witness in our own times. It is only when we follow the way of the Prince of Peace that violence has a chance to cease in this belligerent world. Learn to be at peace this Lent and pray that peace will be a reality in our world.

Lord, make me an instrument of Your peace within this world, so often rent asunder by violence, hatred, jealousy and anger. Amen.

HUMILITY

The publican, standing a far off,
would not lift up so much as
his eyes unto heaven, but smote
upon his breast, saying,
'God be merciful to me a sinner.'

Luke 18. 13.

Full Readings: Hosea 5.16-6.6; Psalm 51. 3-4, 18-21; Luke 18. 9-14.

APART FROM LOVE, THE virtue of humility is preached more than any other in the New Testament and by the Fathers and Mystics of successive generations. Our Lord made it very clear that unless we live humbly we would not enter the kingdom of heaven. Our Lord bids us to be last rather than first; and to take the lower place rather than the higher so we don't make ourselves out to be better than others. What our Lord is telling us that if we are to follow Him we must always consider the need and worth of others as well as our own worthiness. Every time we recite the *Magnificat* and ponder on Mary's words, we shall see humility in the right perspective.

When we see and do everything from our own selfish instincts and desires we are committing the sin of pride, the very opposite of humility. The parable of the Publican and Pharisee of course manifests this. The Pharisee's sin was not that he fasted and gave tithes twice in the week, but that he was arrogant about it, and did not see his actions in the context of an expression of love either to God or his fellow man. He failed to recognize God or His goodness. On the other hand the publican saw himself for what he is a wretched man who had fallen short of that image in which he was created.

Humility is essentially giving worth where it is due. If we acknowledge that all that we have in goods and talents come from God then we automatically give Him the praise for whatever we have. Furthermore if God has given us such riches, it should make us realize that He also gives gifts to others. Thus we are able to rejoice with our brothers and sisters in their achievements and to respect the dignity of our fellow human beings. In this way we come to see ourselves in the right perspective and less likely to commit the sin of pride, which is putting "I" before others and in place of others. In fact if we put ourselves first, we take from God or our neighbour what is due to them; and setting ourselves up as a god.

Yet at times we are tempted to be proud and even boastful about our achievements. Worse still we sometimes gloat over them even to the detriment of others. Sobering it is then to recall that the sin of pride is the root of all evil; it was the cause of Adam's fall, and it is the sin which leads to many other sins. The first Petrine letter reminds us to "humble yourselves ... under the mighty hand of God, (1 Pet. 5.6), and James speaks in a similar vein, "Humble yourself in the sight of the Lord" (Jam. 4.10) while Paul instructs us to "put on ... humbleness of mind" (Col. 3.12). Therefore it is necessary for us to pray continually for grace to overcome the sins of pride, self-centredness, selfish desires and arrogance. Lent is a wonderful time to embrace humility. If we try to practice humility, we are rewarded with the sense of freedom. There is never any thought of comparing or wanting to be as good as someone else. One is free to be the person God wants him or her to be, and the only thing that really matters is to be that person. Trying to be humble also enables us to manifest those other fruits of the Spirit within our lives more easily. We find that patience, tolerance, compassion and understanding come more readily.

If we still have difficulty in clothing ourselves in humility or at least edging closer to it, this Lent is a time to reflect on the greatest example of humility, God becoming man, God living as we do, experiencing the pain, the heartache, as well as the joy. Andrewes expresses God's humility as: "Love, not only condescending to take our nature upon Him, but to take it by the same way and after the same manner that we do, by being conceived. ... The womb of the Virgin ... He might well have abhorred,... [but] He stayed ... nine months." In another of his Nativity sermons, he took Christ's birth to emphasize the need for Christians to practise humility.

> There lies He, the Lord of glory without glory. Instead of a palace, a poor stable, of a cradle of state, a beast's cratch; no pillow but a lock of hay; no hangings but dust and cobwebs; no attendants, but in 'medio animalium'. ...
>
> Christ, though as yet He cannot speak as a new born babe, yet by it He speaks, and out of His crib, as a pulpit, this day preaches to us; and his theme is ... 'Learn of Me for I am humble' - humble in My birth you all see. ...
>
> For the word of God has two edges; and if it go one way thus for humility, it cuts as deep the contrary against pride. And withal, under one leads us to the cause straight, and shows us the malignity of the disease of pride, for the cure whereof this so profound humility was requisite in Christ. ...
>
> For if humility be the sign of finding Christ, pride must needs be the sign of losing Him; and who so loses Him, is himself even the child of perdition; and therefore look to this sign well.[67]

During Lent let us take Andrewes' advice and loathe the vice of pride, so that growing in humility we may be able to see Christ and His teaching more clearly.

Dear Lord, teach me to learn from Your examples of humility through Your earthly life so that each day I can die a little more to pride and self. Amen.

---

67 Andrewes, Vol. 1, pp. 140, 204 - 7.

THE FOURTH SUNDAY IN LENT

(or Laetere Sunday or Mothering Sunday)

REFRESHMENT

You prepared a table for me in
the presence of my enemies; you anoint
my head with oil; my cup runs over.

Psalm 23. 5.

Full Readings:

Cycle A: 1 Samuel 16.1, 6-7, 10-13; Psalm 23; Ephesians 5. 8-14; John 9.1-41.

Cycle B: 2 Chronicles 36.14-16, 19-23; Psalm 136; Ephesians 2. 4-10; John 3.14-21.

Cycle C: Joshua 5. 9-12; Psalm 33; 2 Corinthians 5.17-21; Luke 15.1-3, 11-32.

THIS MIDDLE SUNDAY IN Lent has many names: *Laetare* Sunday, Refreshment Sunday, and in England and Commonwealth countries also Mothering Sunday. *Laetare* Sunday comes from the opening word of the introit "Rejoice". To denote this rejoicing and refreshing the celebrant wears rose coloured vestments (as he does on *Gaudete* Sunday in Advent). It was known as Refreshment Sunday in the old calendar as the Gospel for this Sunday was the feeding of the five thousand. On a green hillside in Palestine families were refreshed and nourished by bread as indeed we are at the Eucharistic banquet. Accordingly in the past the Church encouraged its people to refresh themselves on this middle Sunday in order to continue their rigid fasting for the rest of Lent and Holy Week. The man blind from birth in today's Gospel certainly knew what it was to be renewed and refreshed as Christ gave him sight.[68]

It is also a fitting day to be kept as Mothering Sunday when we remember our three mothers. The Church, our spiritual Mother refreshes us through the Blessed Sacrament, while our earthly mothers have refreshed us over and again, not just in feeding us but also by comforting and sustaining us in so many ways. Many will recall the times, for example, when Mother stayed with us in the night when we were ill or frightened by a dream or the dark. And of course our blessed Mother Mary who prays for us and who has set us the example of obedience to God and devotional love to her Son. So on this day we all have much to be thankful for as God has provided for us abundantly.

Returning to this Sunday being an interlude in our Lenten journey, it also should serve as a reminder of our entire life as a pilgrimage to the heavenly city. It is a long journey, fraught with many dangers, weariness, loneliness, uncertainties, and doubts. Yet it is not done alone. Our Lord bids us to stop awhile, to leave our bundle on the road side, and come and rest with Him "in a green pasture" by "the waters of comfort".

He is "the good Shepherd" who will "feed His flock", and gently "gather the lambs with His arm, and carry them in His bosom" (Is. 40.11). When we are weary, from the pace some of us live to-day, how often do we express the sentiments of the Psalmist, "O that I had wings like a dove: for then would I flee away, and be at rest" (Ps.55.6). It is at such times that this image of Christ being a Shepherd who tenderly looks after us is so refreshing. To collapse into a chair as it were, and let God take over for a few minutes gives us strength to get up again and continue with work and life in general. Those few minutes resting in Him are as refreshing as the early morning dew on the grass. We are assured that "they who wait upon the Lord … renew their strength" (Is. 40.31).

I think we all need to rest in the Lord occasionally. In a city full of noise where we have spent a morning shopping, how refreshing it is to enter a church; it is a sanctuary of quietness, coolness and blessedness as we sit and rest away from it all. However being refreshed is

---

68 See Friday after the Second Sunday in Lent for an account of this.

not to be confused with or replace contemplation. It is essentially a harbour where we anchor for awhile to regain that vigour needed to press on again. "Cast your burden upon the Lord, and He will nourish you" (Ps. 55.22). We surrender our weariness and problems into His hands and relax knowing that God's presence is soothing, and we shall get up refreshed enough to carry on.

The last office of the day, Compline, prays for this kind of rest during the night as we commend our being into His hands. One of the set Psalms tells us, "He will defend you under His wings, and you will be safe under His feather: His faithfulness and truth will be your shield and buckler" (Ps. 91.4). If we don't say the entire Compline Office at the end of the day, many Christians will commend themselves into His care, and say one of the versicles of this Office, "Into your hands I commend my spirit", and the canticle, *Nunc Dimittis* with its antiphon, "Save us while waking and guard us while sleeping, that awake we may be with Christ, and in sleep we take our rest."

So this Refreshment and Mothering Sunday rest in our Lord by being refreshed by the Heavenly Food at the altar as well as our special celebrative meal with our dear mother and family, knowing that our blessed Mother is praying for us. Then we shall begin the second part of Lent with renewed vigour.

Dear Saviour, as You refreshed Your people of old by giving them manna, so sustain me with the Bread which comes down from heaven. Amen.

PRAISE

Sing unto the Lord, O you saints.

Psalm 30. 4.

Full Readings: Isaiah 65. 17-21; Psalm 30. 2-6, 11-13; John 4. 43-54.

TODAY'S READINGS EXPRESS JOY, praise and thanksgiving for what God has done in healing the centurion's son and the Israelites' safeguard against the enemies and the hope that comes from both accounts.

Praising God I think is the easiest form of praying as our world is a glorious manifestation of God's beauty, grandeur, purity and loveliness. The Jesuit poet, Gerard Manley Hopkins, captured this in the opening lines of these two sonnets:

> The world is charged with the grandeur of God.
> It will flame out, like shining from shook foil;
> It gathers to a greatness, like the ooze of oil
> Crushed.

and

> Glory be to God for dappled things-
> For skies of couple-colour as a brinded cow;
> For rose-moles all in stipple upon trout that swim;
> Fresh-firecoal chestnut-falls; finches' wings;
> Landscape plotted and pierced-fold, fallow, and plough;
> And all trades, their gear and tackle and trim.[69]

---

69 Hopkins, *God's Grandeur*, p. 26, *Pied Beauty*, p. 30.

When we behold the created in all its splendour, how more splendid must be the Creator. The summit of all creation must be the heavenly Jerusalem to which our earthly pilgrimage is leading us. Here beholding this beatific vision are already the whole hosts of angels - "seraphs, cherbubim and thrones, ... dominions, princedoms, powers, virtues, archangels, [and] angels" who sing their praises unceasingly. We mortals here on earth are bidden to take up the angels' hymn of praise, so His glory can echo in every part of the world.

So each day we praise God for His creation all around us, "O Lord, how manifold are your works: in wisdom have you made them all; the earth is full of your riches" (Ps.104.24). In springtime this is not too difficult to do. And it is not too difficult either when our eyes behold the Grand Canyon for the first time or Cappadocian fairy chimneys or the Jungfrau peak in the Swiss Alps. Yet it is for the ordinary things of life, the everyday things we take almost for granted that we also have to be able to offer up our praises to God. Hence we should praise Him for the new day and the opportunities it will bring. If we think the day is going to be difficult recall our blessings. We have a voice to praise Him, a heart to lift up to Him and hands to reach out to Him. Whenever we want to complain, think what we do have rather than what we do not have and praise our Creator for those good things daily. That turns our minds outward, away from self and enables us to get life in the right perspective again.

One of the reasons I like using the Psalms as a source of meditation is that the Psalter bubbles over with such outburst as this last verse of Psalm 103, "O speak good of the Lord, all you works of His, in all places of His dominion: praise you the Lord, O my soul." The Psalter in forming a dominant part of the Daily Offices remind and help us in our daily praises to God as the canticles do too, for these are essentially songs of praise. The glorious words of the *Te Deum*, or the *Magnificat* should never be far from our lips.

I cannot think of a better way to conclude but in the words of that gentle Caroline Divine, George Herbert who in his own life lived a life of praise, and through his poetry has enabled us to share in His praising God.

Seven whole days, not one in seven,
    I will praise Thee:
In my heart, though not in heaven,

I can raise Thee. ...

Small it is, in this poor sort
>   To enrol Thee:
E'en eternity's too short
>   To extol Thee.[70]

O blessed Saviour, let everything within me praise Your holy name and especially as I greet each new day. "Praise the Lord, O my soul; while I live will I praise the Lord: yes, as long as I have any being, I will sing praises unto my God" (Ps. 146.1-2). Amen.

---

70 Dorman, p. 20.

PETITIONS

'Will you be made whole?'

John 5. 6.

Full Readings: Ezekiel 47. 1-9, 12; Psalm 46. 2-9; John 5.1-3, 5-16.

IT HAS ALWAYS PUZZLED me why this paralytic man who lay near the pool of Bethzatha for those thirty-eight years never cried out for someone to help him into the stirring water. On the other side of the coin he was completely ignored by others who came to the pool. When Christ neared the pool the paralytic learnt he did not need this water but only Christ Himself.

It would seem he never prayed to God for strength or courage either, what we call petitionary prayer, that is, when we pray for our own needs. Just as thanksgiving and praise are closely bound, so are petitionary and intercessory prayers. We perceive that God knows our petitions before we pray them, but nevertheless He wants to hear our asking for them. "Lord, I call upon you, haste you unto me: and consider my voice when I cry unto you" (Ps.141.1).

Our petitions form part of our Morning Prayer as we place our various needs and circumstances for that day before God. These include asking for divine grace to know His will and strength to do it. If we are having any special problems at work or home we ask God especially for His gifts of love, peace and healing so that we can endeavour to improve these situations. Then there are those days when we have to venture into the unknown, and we feel a little scared of the uncertainty so we pray for courage and trust.

However we should not bombard God with our petitions. Petitionary prayers, like our intercessory ones, once offered to God in the morning, should be left with Him. This does not include of course those unknown situations which arise doing the course of any day. In these circumstances we should turn to God immediately and seek His help. We do this by offering up an arrow prayers, often very simply expressed, "Help me here dear Lord." As Christians we do have to believe that "all things work together for good to them who love God" (Rom. 8.28).

When we are taught about prayer in our Confirmation class we are invariably told that petitionary prayer comes last; and when our fingers represent each type of prayer, our little finger represents this kind. Just as in our everyday living, God and others are more important than ourselves, so in prayer. Indeed if we have petitionary prayer in its right perspective, it should help us to overcome our selfish nature, and to look outward rather than inwards.

Petitionary prayers are also interwoven with the Church's fasts and feasts. For example at Pentecost we pray for the Spirit to possess us so that we radiate His goodness in all we do or think or say. At this time too we pray for the fruits of the Spirit such as love, peace, patience, long-suffering, compassion and tolerance. During this season of Lent we pray to use this special time to draw closer to our blessed Saviour so that we may more easily follow our Lord to Jerusalem, and enter into His passion.

Lent is a valuable time to use petitionary prayer to subdue our wills to His, so that it is He who is living and speaking through us. "O sacred heart of Jesus, I offer you my life" is the perfect prayer for each day.

Dear God help me to pray for what I need for my daily living but above all give me sufficient grace to be the person You want me to be. Amen.

Joy

Sing O heavens: and be joyful.
Isaiah 49.13.

Full Readings: Isaiah 49. 8-15; Psalm 145. 8-18; John 5. 17-30.

BASKING IN THE SUNLIGHT of God's love and soaking up His infinite bounties of grace and goodness as well as being surrounded by the beauties of His creation, cannot but fill one with tremendous joy and praise. "I will sing unto the Lord as long as I live: I will praise my God while I have my being" (Ps.104.33). A crisp, white morning with the frost sparkling in the sunshine and an exquisite sunset are just two examples that bring a joyful response.

Perhaps Farindon had Isaiah's reading for today in mind when he preached, "If love be as the sun, joy and delight are the beams which stream forth from it. If love be as the voice, joy is the echo; for joy is but love in the reflection."[71] When I recall my happy days in Oxford there were many times I would cycle back to my flat, especially on Sundays or Feasts days after a glorious High Mass, just brimming over with delight and joy from experiencing the worshipping of God in the beauty of holiness.

Worship is indeed a time to be full of joy. Andrewes saw each major festival as expressing this. For example, Christmas "is news of joy", Good Friday is "the joy of our salvation" and Easter is the day of "joyful tidings". As God has done something special for us on each Christian festival our joy should abound in recognition of His birth,

---

71 Farindon, Vol. 1, pp. 255-6.

death and resurrection. Therefore for those who are thankful for Our Lord becoming man, dying and rising for our salvation, "there is no joy in the world to the joy of a man saved; no joy so great, no news so welcome, as to one ready to perish, in case of a lost man, to hear of one [who] save him."[72] Indeed when the priest says to the penitent, "Go in peace, the Lord has taken away your sins", there is always an overwhelming joy. Being released from anything is always an occasion of joy, but most especially from sin.

When we are over brimming with joy we experience something of the angelic delight in heaven where they sing their praises unceasingly to their Creator. As the angelic hosts always surround the altar at every Eucharist, we join them in their unending praise, especially at the Sanctus. We can share their joy too when we approach the altar to receive our dear Lord in the Blessed Sacrament. Indeed our attitude towards attending the Sunday Eucharist should be like that of the Jews as they ascended the temple singing the Psalm, "I was glad when they said to me: We will go into the house of the Lord."

Thus every Sunday is a special day of joy, as we celebrate Christ's Resurrection, evident in this sermon of another Caroline Divine, John Cosin. "This ... joy is so expedient and natural for a festival solemnity that without it, it seems no feast at all." Sunday is indeed a day of "joy and cheerfulness."[73]

Of course every day brings its own joy if we but choose it - a new day with its fresh opportunities to give, to share or to make progress in work or relationship. There are also the unexpected joys of little things such as receiving a letter from our family, or a telephone call from a friend we have not heard from for ages, or the warmth exchanged in greetings while walking the dog or going for a run in the park, or somebody being very kind to us when out shopping.

But perhaps our greatest joy is when we do things consciously or even unconsciously for our dear Lord. There are so many ways we can do this, ranging from an act of self-denial to visiting the lonely person down the road or the homebound. We cannot read the twenty-fifth chapter of Matthew's Gospel without being conscious of the various ways we minister to Christ. Perhaps like the saints of old we are not called upon to die joyfully the martyr's death, but every time we say "no" to self and "yes" to Him, it is a victory for Christ.

---

72 Andrewes, Vol. 1, pp. 66, 73, Vol. 2, p. 176, Vol. 3, p. 9.
73 Cosin, Vol. 1, pp. 186-7.

For Christians there is also the joy of expectancy, of waiting for that glorious moment when we shall at last see Him. Then Our Lord Jesus will reveal to us all the joys of heaven. That joy will be almost indescribable, as expressed here by Charles Wesley.

> Those dear tokens of His passion
> > Still His dazzling body bears,
> Cause of endless exultation
> > To His ransomed worshippers:
> > > With what rapture
> Gaze we on those glorious scars.[74]

Being joyful in our worship, faith, attitude and work starves inertia and disappointment. Without joy our souls will wither, like a dried-up carrot left forgotten in a refrigerator. Let joy be part of your life this Lent.

Dear Lord, let each day be an occasion to rejoice and be glad as it brings its own newness, beauty and hope. Fill me with such holy joy that even in my darkest and dreariest moments that sense of joy may always flicker within me. Amen.

---

74 *New English Hymnal*, p. 14.

REMORSE

The Lord said unto Moses, 'Go, get you down:
for your people, whom you brought out of the
land of Egypt have corrupted themselves.'

Exodus 32. 7.

Full Readings: Exodus 32. 7-14; Psalm 106. 19-23; John 5. 31- 47.

BOTH THE OLD AND New Testament readings today reveal how little remorse the Israelites had in breaking the Commandments given to them by Yahweh at Mt. Sinai, so soon after their release from slavery in Egypt. Years later in the time of Our Lord they were still refusing Moses' teaching.

The closer we try to live with God and let Him work through us the more conscience we become of what our sinning does to His Son. We truly realize that sin grieves His sacred heart very much, that heart which broke at Golgotha as He bore the sin of mankind. In such contemplation our hearts respond to the despicableness of our sins. In our wretchedness we cry out from the depth of our being:

> Cease not, wet eyes,
> His mercies to entreat.
> ...
> Nor let his eye
> See my sin, but through my tears.[75]

---

75   Ibid., p. 127.

This is what the Fathers called the sacrament of *lachrymæ*. We weep for our sins; we groan for them; we mourn for them. We know we deserve only the everlasting flames of hell because of them. In a sense our wretchedness is made worse because we realize that God's mercy is such that He has forgiven us almost before we confess our sins. He is ever awaiting us with outstretched loving arms. No wonder hot, bitter tears drop, drop when we ponder our sins. Like Peter, the impact of sin makes us weep bitterly.

Remorse is also part of our spiritual growth as witnessed by many of the saints who saw this as being instrumental in their growing awareness and closeness to God. However it is a feature of our Christian life, if it grows out of proportion to other aspects, it makes us gloomy and morbid Christians. That I do not think we are meant to be. We are also called to be joyful people as we saw yesterday, but yet we cannot feel real joy without knowing remorse.

Yet Lent is a good time to feel emotionally the depth of the wrongness of sin, if we never have experienced it before. If we cannot be moved within ourselves, may I suggest we kneel in front of a crucifix and gaze and gaze on it, and in the silence let every aspect of our Lord's agony penetrate our souls. You will respond to such Love as illustrated in this Good Friday sermon of Andrewes.

> It was the sin of our polluted hands that pierced His hands, the swiftness of our feet to do evil that nailed His feet, the wicked devices of our heads that gored His head, and the wretched desires of our hearts that pierced His heart. ...
>
> Look upon Him and pierce; and pierce that in you, that was the cause of Christ's piercing; that is sin and the lusts thereof. ... Look and be pierced with love of Him, who so loved you, that He gave Himself in this sort to be pierced for you. ... Look upon Him, and His heart opened, and from that gate of hope promise yourself, and look for all manner of things that good are: ... the deliverance from the evil of our present misery ... [and] the restoring to the good of our primitive felicity. ... Look and look for; by the Lamb who is pierced to be freed from all misery, by the High Priest who is pierced fruition of all felicity. ... Look back upon it with some pain; for one way or other, look upon it we must.[76]

---

76 Andrewes, Vol. 2, pp. 126, 131-33, 135.

So this Lent let the cross pierce our very being so we respond positively to it.

Heavenly Father I offend you every time I sin. Let me mourn for my sins that caused Your Son's death, and with Your grace to amend my life once I have confessed them. Amen.

DEATH

Let us condemn him with a shameful death:
for by his own saying he will be respected.

Wisdom 2. 20.

Full Readings: Wisdom 2.1, 12-22; Psalm 34. 16-23; John 7.1-2, 10, 25-30.

THE FIRST READING TODAY predicts the kind of death Christ would endure, while in the second John makes clear Christ's death would be His hour of glory as He accomplished the will of the Father. His dying thus took the sting out of death, the punishment for Adam's sin as Paul outlined in 1 Corinthians (15.55).

Christians no longer have to fear death thanks to Christ. It is the gateway to a better life, an eternal life and therefore we should live each day as if it were our last in preparation for it. This means we strive to live in a state of grace, and have made adequate arrangements about our earthly ties so as not to give any more burdens to our families. We should be as considerate in death as in life.

Death as the gateway to that fuller and richer life will lead us to our celestial home where we shall behold the beatific vision, and in spontaneous response fall down and worship our blessed Lord. Seen in the Christian light, death is a joyful occasion and therefore there is nothing morbid or hush-hush about it. As the saintly Bishop Ken wrote, "Teach me to live, that I may dread/ The grave as little as my bed."[77]

Sadly though, many people, even Christians have a fear of death,

---

77 *New English Hymnal*, p. 371.

one could say almost a repulsion of it these days. This is evident so clearly in our hospitals when people are kept alive on machines, just to starve off death. The days are rapidly disappearing when our loved ones die at home surrounded by priest and family. As a result most people do not want to ponder about dying, but if they would, they would see death not as an end but a welcome to a better life. The beloved Son has assured us of this with these words, "I go to prepare a place for you, ... that where I am, there you may be also" (Jn 14.2). Then we are always ready to die, and we do not have to behave like an ostrich with its head in the sand.

In the midst of life is death, and we all have experienced the sudden death of someone close to us whether by accident or illness. We too may die like that, and that is why in one of the petitions in the Church's Litany we pray that we may be delivered from "sudden death". It is comforting to think of death coming to us after our "three score years and ten" and being able to live each day preparing for it, in the security that "Love [bids] me welcome". But often it is not like that as Our Lord assured us that "we do not know the time or the hour." Therefore we must make sure that we don't make the same mistake as the rich man did who spent his time on building bigger and better buildings so he could live more comfortably without any thought for his soul. Our Lord's teaching in this parable is sobering, "You fool, this night your soul shall be required of you" (Lk.12.20). As the late Metropolitan Anthony of Sourozh reminds us, "It is only if we face death, make sense of it, determine its place and our place in regard to it, that we will be able to live in a fearless way and to the fullness of our ability."[78]

Physical death is a deliverance - a deliverance from our continual strivings to conquer sin, and being released into the nearer presence of God. Donne certainly saw death as a deliverance when he stated, "This *exitus mortis*, the issue of death, is *liberatio in morti*, a deliverance in death; not that God will deliver us from dying but that He will have a care of us in the hour of death, of what kind soever our passage be." Our deliverance from death is achieved:

> First, as the God of power, the Almighty Father rescues His servants from the jaws of death: And then as the God of mercy, the glorious Son rescued us, by taking upon Himself the issue of

---

78 Bloom, p. 8.

death: And then between the two, as the God of Comfort, the Holy Spirit rescues us from all discomfort by His blessed impressions before hand.

Donne assures us however we die, death itself will "be an entrance into everlasting life." This is the hope through all "our deaths and deadly calamities of this life, ... [in] all our periods and transitions in this life."[79]

As well as our physical death, there is also the spiritual to consider during Lent. This is being cut off from God when we perpetually live in sin and do nothing about it. However for Christians life is a series of deaths and risings. We sin but when we are truly penitent we are restored to a life of grace. Furthermore every time we say "no" to self and "yes" to Him we have triumphed over death and grow in holiness. Hence we either die to sin or sin deadens us. There is no other alternative.

During this Lent let us live so that like St. Francis we are always ready to welcome death as our dear sister: "Praise be to you, my Lord, through our Sister, Bodily Death, from whom no living man can escape."[80]

By Your passion and resurrection O Lord, death has no more dominion over us. Help me to live each day as if it were my last in preparation for the fuller life in Your nearer presence. Amen.

---

79 Donne, *Twenty-six Sermons*, pp. 397 - 8.
80 St. Francis, p. 4.

SATURDAY AFTER THE FOURTH SUNDAY IN LENT
___

THE BLESSED SACRAMENT

*Many of the people therefore, when they heard this
saying, said, Of a truth this is the prophet.'*

John 7. 40.

Full Readings: Jeremiah 11. 18-20; Psalm 8.2-3, 9-12; John 7. 40 - 53.

THE ABOVE PROCLAMATION WAS made on the last day of the feast of
Tabernacles after our Lord had declared, "Let anyone who is thirsty
come to me, and let the one who believes in me drink." In John's Gospel Christ's appearing at this festival followed after the feeding of the
Five Thousand and His discourse on being the Bread of Heaven. "I
am the living bread which came down from heaven: if any man eat
of this bread, he will live for ever: and the bread that I will give is my
flesh, which I shall give for the life of the world" (Jn 6.51).

One of the advantages of being a Catholic Christian is that we
have plenty of opportunities of visiting Christ in the Blessed Sacrament and spending time with Him in this special way. One of the
resolutions we make for Lent is to do this more often and attend
more often daily Mass. Countless numbers of Christians reverently
receive Him under the veil of Bread and Wine each day. For them it
is the summit of everything done that day as they reach out with outstretched hands to receive Him. This is the most wonderful way to be
assured of Christ within us. As we sing most joyously in the Corpus
Christi procession or sometimes after Benediction:

Blessed and praised be Jesus Christ

98

In the most holy Sacrament.
Hosanna, hosanna, hosanna in the highest!

Oh, what joy at that moment when we receive the Sacrament and we wish that moment would linger. John Evelyn of Wotten, writing during the seventeenth century when the English liturgy was forbidden to be celebrated by Parliament, captures something of this moment. "For [it] is certain, that the most precious moments of our lives are those which immediately precede or succeed the participation of the Holy Eucharist. For before, we strive to fit and prepare ourselves to receive our Lord, and afterwards to keep possession of Him."[81] A contemporary of Evelyn, Cosin, once said if we only realized we were receiving our Lord at the altar rails, we would run to it. Oh, Lord, let me run so that I may "ever adore You in the most holy Sacrament of the altar."

We are never as close to Christ as we are at that moment "when we have newly taken the holy Sacrament of His blessed Body and most precious Blood - when we come fresh from it," Andrewes assured us.[82] His closeness is what every earnest Christian desires. We do not want to be parted from Him, and in our better moments we wish to be with Him for ever. We want to say as Kronstadt of modern times stated, "Oh perfect love! Oh all-embracing love! Oh strongest love! What shall we give God in gratitude for this love?" That is why Benediction is so appealing and devotional to so many Christians. We want continually to "taste and see how glorious the Lord is", and stay in "our true native land".[83] Our preparation and thanksgiving become even more important.

In our preparation, "Just as the watchman waits for the morning, so I wait for You O Lord", and "My soul thirsts for God, even for the living God" become powerful words from the Psalms. Yes, Lord I do wait upon You, and I do thirst after You. After all to whom should I go, You have the words of eternal life? As equally important is our thanksgiving after receiving the Blessed Sacrament. How can we ever thank God enough for what He gives us each day? We cannot. But we can try and let Christ shine through after we leave the church as an expression of our gratitude. After all, as already men-

---

81 Evelyn, p. 13.
82 Andrewes, Vol. 1, p. 214.
83 Kronstadt, *Life*, p. 35.

tioned elsewhere He has no other feet or hands or even heart to do His work except ours.

Another wonderful aspect of being present at the daily Eucharist is that we know at that moment we are united with our fellow Christians throughout the world. We are all part of the Body of Christ, the Christian community, and for those of us who live a long distance from our families, the moment of Communion bond us with our loved ones. Moreover it makes us more aware of the brotherhood of mankind. As we are all God's children, and one in Christ, it should help us to not only to pray for all our brothers and sisters but also to work against the various injustices inflicted on many. In the Liturgy of St. Basil the Great this unity in Christ as brothers is emphasized in this prayer.

> O God our heavenly Father, we pray Thee to unite us all who partake of the one Bread and of the Chalice, to one another in the Communion of Thy One Holy Spirit; and may none of us, who receive the Holy Body and Blood of your Christ, receive Them to our judgment or our condemnation; but may we all find mercy and grace with all the Saints who have ever pleased You, and with every righteous soul made perfect in the Faith. Amen.[84]

What more could our blessed Lord do to encourage us to His Banquet than what He has done in teaching us that He is the Bread of Life; He is Life itself! Thus:

> He bids us come without money and without price to the waters of life: He came Himself to seek the lost sheep and bear it on His shoulders. Not satisfied with all this, He sends His Ambassadors to assure us of our peace, no, to entreat us to be reconciled, and His servants sweetly to compel even the most miserably indigent to come in, that His Table may be furnished with guests. O inexhaustible Treasure, never failing Source; Banquet of Love, where the hungry soul is treated with the Bread of Angels and the Manna which descends from heaven. How,

---

84 *Orthodox Manual*, p. 40.

O how should we not thirst after these cooling streams and languish after this precious Food.[85]

Let us this Lent thirst after this living Water and heavenly Bread.

O dearest Lord, let me always be thankful for receiving Your life in the Blessed Sacrament and then sharing that life with others. Amen.

---

85   Evelyn, pp. 12-13.

FIFTH SUNDAY IN LENT

LOVING GOD

Lord, if you had been here my brother had not died.

John 11.21.

Full Readings:

Cycle A: Ezekiel 37.12.14; Psalm 130; Romans 8.8 -11; John 11.1- 45.

Cycle B: Jeremiah 31.31-34; Psalm 51; Hebrews 5. 7-9; John 12.20-33.

Cycle C: Isaiah 43.16-21; Psalm 126; Philippians 3.18-14; John 8.1-11.

MARTHA'S WORDS REVEALED HOW much she loved Jesus and believed that if He had been present her brother would not have died. Her sister, Mary, echoed the same belief. Christ loved them too and wept upon hearing this news of Lazarus death.

When Christ raised him from the dead after four days it was the climax of the seven signs in John's Gospel, and thus a fitting end for the first part. After this miracle when our Lord manifests Himself as Lord even of the dead, the Gospel turns to the Passion. In the old calendar to-day was known as Passion Sunday, which made that turning more real than just calling this Sunday the Fifth Sunday in Lent.

Accordingly today marks a turning point in our Lenten devotions from focusing on our sins and repentance to the Passion. Just as our Lord set His face towards Jerusalem, so do we. That journey to Jerusalem will take us to Bethany, the garden in Gethsemane, bathed by the Passover moon as an agonized soul struggles with temptation, and eventually to Golgotha, outside the city, where as the day takes on night, a cry penetrates the darkness, "It is finished", or as some translations have it, "It is accomplished."

As we trace this journey, God's love is like a beacon, enlightening us more and more to the extent of that love, a love that condescends to travel the road to Golgotha because of our fallen humanity. When we reach the foot of the cross at the end of our Lenten journey we see the huge cost of that love. Such a journey should make us realize how we fall so short of reciprocating that love. This Passiontide thus gives us another opportunity to grow in love for God as we follow in the Son's footsteps along the dusty road to Jerusalem. Let us be like St. Augustine and bring our hearts with us, and say, "Behold I love, and if it be too little, I would love more strongly."[86] When St. Augustine spoke of our hearts being restless until they find God, this is what he meant. Until we can love God unconditionally for what He is, there will always be an empty and hollow feeling within us. When we do not love God, we sever the natural bond between the Creator and the created.

Journeying along this road, "Love says, *I covet nothing, but one, and that is Jesus,*"[87] as the mediaevalist mystic, Walter Hilton put it or as another contemporary mystic, Richard Rolle expressed it, "I shall rejoice in my Lord through the sweetness of His love, and I shall be glad in God, my Jesus, that is, my Saviour."[88] We can only grow in our love for God by knowing Jesus more and more. That is why Passiontide is such a wonderful opportunity for this growth because if we keep it properly we are walking and praying with, and listening to Jesus on His and our journey to Jerusalem. Pause when He pauses, share His thankfulness to Mary for her lavish gift of love, partake of His last meal with His disciples, watch with Him in the garden and throughout His trial, walk the *via Dolorosa* and lastly stand beside His cross. Such a journey will enable us to live with Christ, and in living with Him to grow in love until we can spontaneously exclaim, "Jesu, my Lord, I you adore, help me to love You more and more". Once we can say that, we find ourselves like Martha and Mary wanting to do things for Him because of our love. Our acts of self-denials, coping with a difficult person, as well as our prayers are all done as an expression of love for Him Who gave all for us. Furthermore in between all our activities we shall want to pause because of our love for

---

86 Augustine, p. 281.
87 Hilton. p. 188.
88 Rolle, p. 180.

Christ make us want to be alone with him quietly for a few minutes constantly throughout the day.

I would like to finish this meditation with St. Bernard of Clairvaux's advice on loving Christ.

> Learn to love Him tenderly, to love Him wisely, to love Him with a mighty powerful love; tenderly, that you be not enticed away from Him; wisely, that you be not deceived and so drawn away from Him; and strongly, that you be not separated from Him by any force. Delight yourself in Christ who is wisdom beyond all else, in order that worldly glory or fleshly pleasure may not withdraw you from Him; and let Christ who is the Truth enlighten you, so that you may not be led away by the spirit of falsehood and error.[89]

My dearest Lord as I follow You to Calvary this Passiontide, give me grace to respond to Your tremendous love by loving You above all things. "Jesus, my Lord I You adore". Amen.

---

89 Bernard, p. 111.

Darkness

Then Suzanna cried out with a loud voice and said,
'O everlasting God, you know the secrets
and know all things before they be:
you know that [these men] have born false
witness against me, and behold I must die.'

Daniel 13. 42.

Full Readings: Daniel 13. 1-9, 15- 17, 19-30, 33-62; Psalm 23; John 8.1-11.

AFTER THE ASSEMBLY HAD condemned the beautiful but virtuous Suzanna to death, darkness must have filled her soul but she found enough courage to exclaim her anguished cry of innocence. The woman taken in adultery must also have looked at that dark pit when she was about to be stoned to a death. Both women however had a saviour – for Suzanna in the young Daniel and for the adulterous woman in Christ. Thus they were spared their darkness through justice or compassion.

Their situations remind us there are times in our lives when there seems only darkness out there, and even inwardly in our souls. Sometimes we echo those words of the Psalmist, "O Lord God of my salvation, I have cried day and night before you: O let my prayer enter into your presence, incline your ear unto my calling" (Ps. 88.1).

I touched on the darkness of the soul in the meditation on Suffering. Today I want to elaborate on what I wrote there because as we grow in the life of prayer we do experience darkness and even deep darkness. As the Psalmist continued in this Psalm, we also exclaim at times: "For my soul is full of trouble: and my life draws nigh unto hell. I am counted as one of them who go down into the pit: ... and lie in the grave: who are out of remembrance, and are cut way from Your hand. You have laid me in the lowest pit: in a place of darkness, and in the deep" (vv. 3–7). The real comfort at such times when everything seems parched is that our Lord knew the intensity of this aloneness. The most desperate plea He made during His life was from the cross when He cried out, "My God, my God, why have You forsaken me?"

We can also draw comfort from the suffering prayers of many of the saints as they struggled against the imprisonment of darkness. We can be sure they too would have echoed this Psalmist's cry: "I am so fast in prison: that I cannot get forth. My sight fails for very trouble: Lord, I have called daily upon you, I have stretched forth my hands unto you" (vv. 8-9).

The author of *A Cloud Unknowing* warned us about darkness as we strive to make contact with our God when he described it like "a cloud unknowing, ... a dark mist which seems to be between you and the light that you aspire unto." Indeed "this cloud" prevents you from either seeing "Him clearly by the light of understanding in your reason", or feeling "Him by sweetness of love in your affection." Thus we must reconcile ourselves to abide in "this darkness" while we ever desire to make contact with our God whom we love."[90]

Some of the saints wrote about darkness in terms of shutting out the world. It was only when the world was dark to the soul that it could then dwell completely on God. Darkness then brought blessing to the soul. Hilton explained how in this darkness of night we can find Jesus. "This darkness and this night [consists] only in the desire and longing after the love of Jesus." Even though this may be for only a short time it is "good and so restful, ... and how blessed it is to feel His love and to be illuminated with His blessed invisible light." This enables us to see the Truth "when the night passes and the day springs."

Elaborating on this, Hilton took Micah's words, "My soul has desired you in the night" and interpreted this to mean. "It is much better to be hid in the dark night ... though it were painful, than to be out in false liking on this world. ... In this darkness you are much nearer to Jerusalem than when you are in the midst of false light." Thus Hilton pleaded, "Therefore apply your heart fully to the strings of grace and

---

90 *Cloud*, p. 8.

use yourself to dwell in this darkness." When you do this "the true light of spiritual knowing will spring up to you." However it will not come "all at once, but secretly ... little by little."

For those who are still "deeply contaminated by sin" this darkness "is at first painful". By perseverance and waiting upon God's grace, Hilton assured such people that their "soul will become so free, strong and recollected it will have no desire to think of anything worldly." Indeed "this darkness will then bring blessing to the soul", because "the desire of the love of Jesus felt in this darkness slays all sins, all fleshly affections and all unclean thoughts" for the present, and hastens our drawing "nearer to Jerusalem." Although we have a long way to travel to Jerusalem, we are given glimpses of this fair city which we shall behold in all its glory when we are perfect.[91]

St. John of the Cross also saw darkness as a prelude to perfection. "The soul must be obscured or deprived of its natural light, that it may be guided by faith to this high end of union." Indeed "the soul draws nearer and nearer to the Divine union in darkness by the way of faith which though it be also obscure, yet sends forth a marvellous light. This darkness may last a very long time."[92]

We must use darkness as period of growth – those times of praying when we don't feel like it, or when we feel abandoned by God. Mother Julian also reminds us that it is those times when we are dry, barren, sick or weak that our prayers are most pleasing to God, even though many a time we find little fulfilment from them.[93] Remain faithful to, and in communion with Him through prayer and the time will come, as the author of *The Cloud Unknowing* assures us, that we shall once again penetrate that darkness and "and beat at that cloud and darkness that is above" us with our darts of longing love.[94] If during this Lent God seems far away, do not despair – He is not; He continues to love us.

My dear Lord, even when I do not feel Your presence within me, help me not to despair but to trust in Your everlasting love. Amen.

---

91   Hilton, pp. 204-5.
92   John of the Cross, Vol. 1, pp. 61-4.
93   Julian of Norwich, p. 134.
94   *Cloud,* p. 29.

TUESDAY AFTER THE FIFTH SUNDAY IN LENT

CONTEMPLATION

When you have lifted up the Son of Man,
then you will know that I am He.

John 8. 28.

Full Readings: Numbers 21. 4-9; Psalm 102. 2-3, 16-21; John 8. 21-30.

THE GOSPEL READING TODAY relates how the Jews did not really want to know who Jesus is. But as Christians we should. The highest plain on which we can communicate with God and discover who he is, is through contemplation. We must "never cease from spiritual desiring and loving of Him"; we must "always be desiring after Jesus more and more to find Him better," so our mystic Hilton assures us. "To find Him we must, because there is no other joy, nor bliss in heaven or in earth, except in Him."[95] Then we can say with the Psalmist "O God. My heart is ready, my heart is ready" (Ps. 108.1).

It is the most energy-giving and concentrated form of prayer we practise. For many of us who already practise contemplation, it is not always easy, we are only saints in the making, and that is why our preparation for it is so important. Hence it is usually undertaken after stilling ourselves and meditating as they form an appropriate preparation for it. We must also leave all our bundles at the foot of the cross and have an ardent desire for Jesus. Then we should be in the right frame of mind to submit our whole being to His presence and give ourselves a chance to hear God and let Him speak to us. In this silence we can seek Him in a silence which is never exhausted.

---

95   Hilton, pp. 68 - 9.

Contemplation for me means soaking in God and absorbing His very fibres as it were. We begin to pierce that cloud unknowing. We seek God and nothing else; we lose ourselves in Him. Sometimes we just want to gaze and gaze upon Him, especially when we contemplate Him before the Blessed Sacrament.

Sometimes it is easier to contemplate and even to pray before an icon or a crucifix. Both I find especially helpful as it always brings its own contemplative response. And there is a benefit of contemplating before a visual aid in that if we do find our mind wandering a glance upon it helps us to return to our task.

To those who ask should we contemplate? I say yes, we must. The world we live in has lost its tranquillity with its noise, bustle and scurry that impound our very existence. In such a world, how are we ever going to hear that still small voice? How are we ever going to learn what is God's will for us? How are we ever going to get to know Him unless we give Him a chance to speak to us? We cannot. That is why it is imperative that we set aside some time each day for the inner life. Like most things in life if we do it around the same time each day, it becomes rooted in that day's activity. If you have never tried or have not been very successful in this aspect of your prayer life, use this Lent to try again and persevere at least until the end of Lent. If you approach it in the right frame of mind, I am sure you will discover a door opening into another world; it's like the mist lifting over the countryside, gradually you see more and more of the foliage, and then suddenly all is clear and beautiful. Furthermore we have the example of our Lord's blessed Mother. If she had not learnt to be still and ponder on eternal things, she would never have been receptive to the voice of the angel, announcing that she would be the God bearer.

If you are starting for the first time, do it only for a short time. You'll probably find that is all you can cope with it. But as you learn to dig deep and deeper into your inner being, you will discover secrets of love and joy you never thought possible, and as you concentrate on God, and as he replenishes you with the living water for your soul, the longer you will want to remain. You will discover you are growing in love with Him. Like the true lover you wish to be alone with the beloved where no words are necessary. The other consideration is to make sure you are comfortable. Being in an uncomfortable position is a distraction and easily becomes the focal point. So adopt that position in which you feel the most at ease. Be warned too that there will be times when God will feel remote and distant, and you won't feel anything but emptiness.

Another reason for contemplation is that we want to live as much like Jesus as we can. When we read the gospels we discover that Jesus spent much time being alone with His Father in prayer. He did this not only to know His will but also to be strengthened to be able to do it. In the Gospel we too have the example of Mary sitting lovingly and silently at the feet of her dear Lord while her sister Martha fussed with her business. The author of *The Cloud Unknowing* describes Mary as rooted to her spot. Nothing would move her, "but sat [completely] still with many a ... sweet stirring of love, cast up to that cloud of unknowing between her and her God." Nothing in the world would desist her from this part.[96]

So by contemplating we are following our Lord's example as well as Mary's. Another reason to consider is that it prepares us for our heavenly task when we shall give unceasingly of our love and adoration to our Lord not now as in the shadow of His glory but in the fullness of it. We shall indeed be in His glorious presence where the light of His countenance shines as perpetual day.

As we draw closer to Holy Week spend time before a crucifix and quietly contemplate on His sufferings until your heart is pierced for love of Him.

My dearest Saviour, fill my heart with such love towards You so that I shall want to spend more and more time being with You in order to get to know You a little better each day. Amen.

---

96 *Cloud*, pp. 64 -5.

Heaven

'Blessed be the God of Shadrach, Meshach,
and Abednego, who has sent his angel,
and delivered his servants who trusted in him.'

Daniel 3. 28.

Full Readings: Daniel 3. 14-20, 24-5, 28; Deuteronomy 3.52-56; John 8.31-42.

THE JEWISH CHILDREN THROWN into the furnace by the heathen king, Nebuchadnezzar, believed that their God would always be with them, and so they lifted up their hearts to heaven and prayed to their God. They knew how more magnificent was their heavenly home in comparison with the earthly, even that of a king.

Heaven is our ultimate home and the purpose of our earthly pilgrimage. Yet on that journey we often stumble and yes, many times fall. Yet the yearning to reach our rightful home, inspired by the Holy Spirit is always with us and led by Him we continue to plod along until, until, until - the ultimate. Here there will be no more weeping, no more sadness, no more dross, but pure joy and ecstasy before the risen and glorified Christ. We shall bathe in that radiant glow and join the angelic choirs in their unceasing alleluias.

In heaven there is perfection, and so we can only be part of that heavenly scene when we have reached the perfect state, that is, when we have been totally transformed into the image of God. That potential is given to us when we are baptized and is continually refined in us by the Spirit until we are no longer tarnished with sin but clothed in holiness. What joy it must be to have the shackles of sin severed for ever!

Heaven is of course sheer loveliness. In one of his Paschal sermons, Andrewes illustrated this splendour of heaven in spring imagery. Earth has a loveliness with its newness of greenery and its blossoms and flowers, but eventually all this will fade, wither and die. However spring in heaven is eternal and perfect with its lushness and loveliness; there "nothing fades, but all springs fresh and green." It is a perpetual spring; "no other season there but that." Furthermore in heaven it is Christ Himself who is the gardener.[97]

In heaven too there is no longer time as we know it - time is timeless. This is because heaven is perfection, a state not contained by time. There we shall be caught up in our praises and gaze upon that glorious site as one eternal moment.

Is it possible to taste heaven while living on earth? I think so. The secret is taste, but not savoured. Those rare times when we live in utter selflessness, when we have completely abandoned ourselves to the Holy Spirit or when we are entirely unconscious of doing a good deed, or when we are completely absorbed in God's presence, give us a glimpse and a feeling of overwhelming joy. Donne was insistent that to "prepare and preserve the joys of heaven" we must taste "joy here [as] this Kingdom of Heaven ... is in us, and [therefore] ... that joy ... is in us."[98]

The Gospel of course tells us that the kingdom of heaven lives within us too. Presumably therefore all those delights which we shall experience perpetually in heaven can be at times touched upon here. Besides joy, there are the experiences of love, beauty, truth, peace, service, selflessness, devotion and wonderment which are eternal. No wonder our Lord told us to seek first the kingdom of God and all things will be given to you! This Lent, as children of the kingdom, let us seek its values with all our heart and soul in order to taste heaven.

O Holy Spirit, finish "Your new creation" in me and make me "pure and spotless" and "perfectly restored in You." Having been

97 Andrewes, Vol. 2, p. 379, Vol. 3, pp. 15-16.
98 Donne, *Fifty Sermons*, pp. 131-2.

"changed from glory into glory" I shall then be ready to take my place in heaven where I shall cast my crown before You "lost in wonder, love and praise." Amen.[99]

---

99   This is based on the last verse of Charles Wesley's hymn, *Love Divine all loves excelling*.

HELL

[The Jews] picked up stones to throw at Jesus.

John 8.59.

Full Readings: Genesis 17. 3-9; Psalm 105. 4-9; John 8. 51-9.

IN THE FIRST READING today we have God making a covenant with Abram which would last forever providing that he and his descendants are faithful to it. However we know that his descendants, the Israelites, broke God's covenant time and time again. The eventual consequences were the destruction of both the northern and southern kingdoms. In the Gospel reading, Jesus Christ, who is the New Covenant, faced denial and hostility from the Jews when He confessed "before Abraham was, I am" (Jn 8.59).

Today when we follow in the same footsteps of the Jews we too cut ourselves from the presence and graciousness of God. Theologically this is what we mean by hell. As the Old and New Testaments show God was loathed to lose His children and gave them chance after chance, until they rejected His promised Son. Why were they and us too so disobedient when God has been so generous to his children?

One of the reasons is because God gave us free-will to accept or refuse His covenant. Each time we break this we sin against God, our neighbours and self. If we do not repent of our sins it leads to a hardening of heart, a deadened soul and living in darkness. This is what Jesus accused the Jews of. It also clogs the channel for the Holy Spirit

Who is our source of goodness. This kind of living is hellish, and we can live in hell now during this earthly life as well as after death.

Our Lord has warned us that on Judgment Day we have to give an account of how we have lived. Those who have done good will have everlasting felicity, and those who have done evil will have everlasting damnation as illustrated in the twenty-fifth chapter of Matthew's Gospel. Christ qualified goodness as living unto Him, manifested in our concern and compassion for others, while evil meant living completely unto self with no thought of God and others. Yet God is merciful and loving and therefore He has warned us of the danger of torment for those who deliberately follow wickedness, rather than goodness. Hammond explained:

> [God] offers not only deliverance from those torments, but over and above, eternal joys upon so easy terms ... that they who will neglect so great salvation proposed to them, with so many advantages and concurrence of all rational motives, and finally make so bad a choice as to take hell as it were by violence, cannot but be thought worthy to take their portion in that lake be it never so punitive and endless.[100]

If we fail to heed God's warnings, then we are casting ourselves eternally away from Him who is Love.

Living in hell denotes we have refused to acknowledge our potential in being renewed and restored to our former glory through the redeeming works of Christ. It is the old Adam who still lives within and not the new. We are a Judas rather than a Peter. Judas' sin in betraying our Lord was not so much the betrayal but in his not repenting and seeking God's forgiveness. So he cast himself into hell as he died unrepentant. Peter on the other hand after his sin of denial, recognized his sin, and wept bitterly in seeking forgiveness. In doing so he was restored and refreshed by the forgiving Spirit. The example of these two disciples illustrates how important it is to live in a state of grace and how devastating unrepentant sin is to the soul. It could mean everlasting separation from God.

There is also the example of Lot's wife, "a relapsing righteous person". She showed the necessity for perseverance in Christian living until the moment we die. Our Lord used her looking back to Zoar

---

100 Fulman, Vol. 1, p. 631.

to show that it was possible for those who have received grace to fall from it, even in the last hours of one's life. The "pillar of salt" is thus a stark reminder that it is possible to be snatched from this life in the process of sinning. Therefore we must be faithful to our life of holiness right unto death if we want to live with God and not away from Him for the rest of eternity. [101]

Hell we know is where the devil and his angels live after having been cast out from heaven. As Satan warred against God in heaven, so he continues this war against Him in us. He wants to drive us away from God and to forget how we were created and for what purpose. He wants us to believe that self is the centre of life rather than God just as to-day's Gospel reading illustrated. Therefore he is always trying to lure us away from the Divine by various temptations. However the whole purpose of Christ's obedience to the Father is to draw us back to God and away from self. If we ignore this, we choose to live with Satan in hell rather than the blessed Trinity in heaven.

One of the questions we have to think seriously about during Lent is how much am I still living with self as the centre of my life. If we are not striving to conquer self little by little each day then we are in danger of living eternity in hell. However as Donne indicated, "There is no necessity that any man, any this or that man should perish ... He does not damn us if we be damned, and we hear Him again speaking for our comfort, we need not be damned at all."[102] All of God's love and mercy will not rescue us from hell if we set up our ego as godlike and usurp God's rightful place. We perish despite God's mercy. This is indeed a sobering thought for us during Lent.

O blessed and holy Trinity, give me grace to fight daily against self and all the vain glories of this world. Teach me to live free from sin by my regular acts of repentance that will fit me for the kingdom of heaven. Amen.

---

101 Andrewes, Vol. 2, p. 62.
102 Donne, *A Sermon*, p. 3.

RISKS

For I hear the defaming of many, fear on every side.
Jeremiah 20.10.

Full Readings: Jeremiah 20.10-13; Psalm 18. 2-7; John 10. 31- 42.

JEREMIAH KNEW WHAT IT was to take risks for his God. Believing that he was delivering God's message to king and people that would save them from destruction from neighbouring armies, he faced persecution, abuse and loneliness. Nevertheless he persevered. The Gospel readings for this week have manifested that Christ too took risks every time He appeared in public as the authorities were seeking His arrest and death. That did not deter Him from His mission to be obedient to the Father's will.

We also have to take risks for Christ in being faithful to Him by standing up for His values and commandments. However I want to reflect on another kind of risk to-day: that risk that comes when we abandon our lives to God, through the power of the Holy Spirit. This is risk magnified. It has nothing to do with security but all with change and the unexpected. The whole essence of being a Christian is to empty ourselves of self, and expose ourselves to God through the working of the Holy Spirit. "I shall pour out my Spirit upon all flesh", we hear on the feast of Pentecost. So I want us to think about the work of the Holy Spirit within us, but to preface it with the Spirit's work within the Trinity.

The Spirit hovers over His creation; He is never still and will not rest until the end of the world. After the initial creation the Father in a sense committed it to the unexpected so that creativity could continue to breathe. St. Augustine explained this combination of the unexpected with creativity as God sowing the seeds, and then allowing them to grow and blossom to their true beings through the Spirit.

We are like those seeds. God has created us with potentiality. That dormant potential has to be unleashed if we are to be the person God wants us to be and to do the things He wants us to do. It means being prepared for the Holy Spirit to prod, quicken and challenge us into action. Through the redeeming works of Christ we have been liberated from our old self, and so we are free to abandon ourselves to the Spirit. Then He can penetrate deeply within because there are no fears, no hesitations, no doubts, and no clinging to impede. Having surrendered, this Spirit will lead us to the unexpected. This is what makes living the Christian life challenging and exciting because we do not know, often from day to day, and indeed from moment to moment where the Spirit will lead us.

It is the Holy Spirit Who also bonds us together in the local community in Christ to discover the gifts we never dreamed we had for communal sharing and enriching. These gifts could be being a lector, a Eucharistic or pastoral minister, a religious educator or a greeter.

The Holy Spirit cannot dwell where there is sin, and so within the soul which ardently seeks Him, He will exude sin. That is, He will be make us so aware of sin and self, that we seek His forgiving grace through confession and our desire to be the person God wants us to be. In undertaking risks we also know that we shall receive the gifts of the Spirit including fearlessness that will enable us to embark on whatever avenue the Spirit directs. These gifts of the Spirit are always at hand, we only have but to ask for them. Then they are given in abundance and we discover that we are an active Christian full of energy and enthusiasm.

If we find ourselves frightened or inactive in Christ's work it should make us look inwards to see what impediments are preventing the Holy Spirit to operate. Are we filled with pride, arrogance, envy, malice, hatred, vengeance etc? If so these sins shut Him out. For the Holy Spirit to work positively within us, we must be humble not proud as Christ was. "Learn of me", He told us. In his 1612 Whitsun sermon, Andrewes preached on this.

One, and a chief one, is pride. For the Holy Spirit will not rest but upon the lowly, says Isaiah; nor God gives grace, but to the humble, says Solomon. ... Therefore pray to Him Who 'gives grace to the humble,' to give us the grace to be humble, that so we may be meet to receive Him. For at His first coming He came 'as a dove', and 'did light upon Him' Who was Himself 'humble and meek,' like a dove, and wills us to learn that lesson of Him, as that which will make us meet to receive the dove which He received, whose qualities are like His, of 'a meek and quiet spirit'; which howsoever the world reckon of it, is with God a thing much set by.

Andrewes also emphasized that another impediment for receiving the Holy Spirit is "carnality" as this is the direct opposite to the spiritual and must be cast out. "The unclean spirit must be cast out, [before] the Holy Spirit received. A clean box it must be that is to hold this ointment. The dove lights on no carrion." [103]

As we approach the most holy of all weeks in the Christian year Andrewes' words give us much on which to ponder.

O Holy Spirit, guide me to be that person You desire. Let me live in harmony with Your Spirit so that day by day it is Christ living within me. Amen.

---

103 Andrewes, Vol. 3, pp. 196-7.

SATURDAY AFTER THE FIFTH SUNDAY IN LENT

TALENT

I will take the children of Israel from the heathens,
whither they be gone, and will gather them on every side,
and bring them into their own lands.

Ezekiel 37. 21.

Full Readings: Ezekiel 37. 21-28; Jeremiah 31. 10-13; John 11.45-56.

WITH MANY INVASIONS OF the Promised Land by various armies from
Assyria and Babylon over two or more centuries many of the Israelites had been dispersed in various parts of the world. The last great
deportation had been after the destruction of Jerusalem in 586 B.C.
when the majority of people were carried off to Babylon by their
captives. About fifty years later under Cyrus, ruler of the Persians,
the Babylonians were defeated and the Israelites were able to return
home. This was Yahweh's doing as reflected in today's first reading.
However to rebuild their beloved city all able men would have to
contribute by using their various talents.

In the Gospels there are various parables told by Jesus about using our talents such as the labourers in the vineyard (Mt. 20.1-16)
and the giving of talents to the three men (Mt. 25. 14- 30). What these
reveal that each of us has been given talents/gifts which must be used
and not squandered.

As Christians we should recognize those gifts which the Holy
Spirit has give us and is continuing to give us and to thank God for
them. The crucial point is to use them the way God would have us
use them. They are a means to glorify Him, and that means they are

120

not to be a show case for our vanities or as a magnet to attract attention to ourselves. Everything that we have we owe to God. It is not I who makes myself clever at a particular task but that creative Spirit working within me. If we have been blessed with outstanding and many gifts, we must remember "that unto whom much is given, much is required", and just as we do have to give an account of our use of time, so we must of the use of our gifts.

Some of us find it difficult to believe that God has given us anything special. We only seem to do very ordinary things day in and day out. Not so. If we find ourselves thinking like this, reflect on who you are. By being created, firstly in the image of God, that in itself gives you gifts, and secondly God has made you differently from anyone else who has lived or will live. You are unique, and no one can do for God what He wants you to do for Him. You are special to Him and that is what counts. Therefore He has given you gifts to do that work for Him. So never think you do not have any talent. You have, and God wants you to use it to be creative and constructive in this world. Don't bury it or hide it or ever be ashamed of it. True humility is to recognize who we really are, and give true worth for what we do through Him. Either of these extremes is sinful: being full of our importance and so called superiority or being full of our unworthiness.

Another misconception is to conceive of gifts as something which has already been given at birth. To believe that is to deny the creativity and operation of the Holy Spirit which not only continues to brood over all creation but is the pulse of it. Thus nothing is static, not even what we consider are our talents in this life. By allowing the Holy Spirit to be creative within us, we are going to discover abilities and gifts of which we never thought we were capable.

If we acknowledge that our gifts and talents come from God, it helps us to live more harmoniously with others. To a certain extent we are like clogs in a big machine in which every clog has its distinctive part in the overall operation. John or Mary working nearby is doing something different from us; it may seem more tedious and not as inspiring on the one hand, or more creative and inspiring on the other, but theirs and our work are all needed for the overall project.

This Lent take time to discover your true gifts, and when you know what they are don't be afraid to spend and be spent. We shall never how much God can use us until we try. Remember He needs us to promote His kingdom in a very secularized world.

O Holy Spirit, continue to refresh and renew me as well as implanting Your gifts. Whatever You give me let me use them as You intend them to be used. Amen.

PALM SUNDAY

CLAMOUR

And the multitudes that went before,
and that followed, cried, saying,
`Hosanna to the son of David; Blessed
is he who comes in the name of the
Lord; Hosanna in the highest.'

Matthew 21.9.

The multitude ... cried out the more,
saying, let Him be crucified.

Matthew 27.23.

Full Readings: Palm Sunday Gospel.
Cycle A: Matthew 21.1-11.
Cycle B: Mark 11.1-10.
Cycle C: Luke 19.28-40.
Mass readings: Isaiah 50. 4-7; Psalm 22; Philippians 2. 6-11.
Cycle A: Matthew 26.14 – 27. 66.
Cycle B: Mark 14.1-15.47.
Cycle C: Luke 22.14-23.56.

HOLY WEEK BEGINS AND ends with demonstrations from the Jews and highlights their fickleness in contrast to the constancy of our Lord. On Palm Sunday our Lord resolves to ride into Jerusalem and exposed Himself publicly, even though He realized the dangers as the Jewish religious leaders were clamouring for His arrest, especially after the raising of Lazarus from the dead. From the Roman Governor's view, this was a dangerous time to keep peace and order with the impending Jewish Passover festival. The last thing the Roman authorities wanted was a riot stirred up by religious fanaticism. So when Christ enters Jerusalem the atmosphere is tense.

As Our Lord set out from the Mount of Olives for the final descent into the holy city people had gathered along the roadside to welcome Him. Many of these had no doubt witnessed His healings, and listened to His preaching, but some perhaps were there to have a glimpse of Christ Who had been causing a stir by His rather radical teaching. As crowds go this would not have been much different from any other crowd then and ever since. The majority found themselves going along with the general consensus, which was to acknowledge joyfully Jesus as a king. Yet within five days the consensus changed. The Jewish religious leaders had no difficulty in relying on mob hysteria and fickleness. There was something better in the air for them on Good Friday or so they thought!

The central figure of Palm Sunday is of course Our Blessed Lord despite the clamour from the crowd. His teaching on this day is simple for His followers, but difficult for many - peace - illustrated by riding into Jerusalem on a donkey rather than a horse. The Prince of Peace proclaims His kingdom in which there is no violence, retaliation, and retribution. Two wrongs never make a right under any circumstance in His kingdom. Palm Sunday teaches us to absorb all the hurts and heartaches of life, otherwise peace will never reign in us or in the world. Thus peace comes from turning the other cheek, going the extra mile and giving and giving of self and time to others until we are drained just as our Lord was drained for us.

So Palm Sunday gives us the opportunity to examine our own faithfulness to Christ. On this wonderful day when we process and wave our palm branches and take our palm crosses home for yet another year, it is all so easy to be caught up with the excitement of it all and get carried along by the very moving Palm Sunday liturgy. The test comes the next day. Are we prepared to stay with Our Lord in Jerusalem as the atmosphere changes towards Him? Do we dare to stand by Him as He faces constant conflict with the religious leaders? Do we love Him enough to want to bathe His weary feet? Do we stay with Him in prayer in the Garden? Are our bodies and souls drained as He dies on the Cross? All these encounters should be included in our cry of "Hosanna to the Son of David: Blessed is He comes in the name of the Lord" today.

As well as Palm Sunday piercing our souls for faithfulness for the whole of this Holy week, it also should pierce our consciences in regards to our overall faithfulness. Again like Palm Sunday festivities, it is rather easy to strive towards holiness when everything seems to be going well but when the bolt out of the blue strikes, what then? When we have to suffer endlessly, whether through physical or spiritual pain, especially if it is inflicted on us by others, what then? When God seems far removed from us and all is dark and despondent, what then? When life seems empty and aimless, what then? Has our faith rooted itself deeply enough to help us cope with these situations, so that they do not control us? Can we see such situations as growing times in holiness or better still more Christ-like? Or are we fickle?

Use this Holy Week as a growing time in faithfulness to Christ, so you will be there at the foot of the cross on Good Friday.

Dear Saviour, I welcome You this day with my palm branch and song of "Hosanna" as the Prince of Peace. Make me an instrument of peace amongst those with whom I live. Amen.

HOLY MONDAY

ANOINTING AND CLEANSING

Mary took a pound of ointment of spikenard,
very costly and anointed the feet of Jesus,
and wiped them with her hair.

John 12. 3.

Full Readings: Isaiah 41. 1-7; Psalm 27. 1-3, 13-4; John 12. 1-11.

JOHN IS EXPLICIT THIS event took place six days before the Passover
and before our Lord entered Jerusalem on what we call Palm Sunday.
Mark placed it within the Passion narrative by having this anointing
taking place two days before the Passover, while Luke has it occur-
ring some time earlier in the ministry. John stated that it took place in
the home of Lazarus and Martha and Mary at Bethany, and it is Mary,
the one who sat at our Lord's feet listening to His words on a previ-
ous visit, who lavishly anointed her Master in anticipation of His
burial. John's version also has overtones of Luke's version of the sinful woman who in breaking her flask of alabaster oil manifested how
generous she was to the Master who forgave her sins. Is John then
hinting that although Christ is the triumphant Messiah, He is about
to die for the sin of mankind? Mark's version also has an anonymous
woman who anoints Christ's head in the home of Simon of Bethany.

Whoever the woman was, although I like to think it is Mary, she
is highly recommended by Christ for her loving deed. Mark recorded
"Truly I tell you: wherever the gospel is proclaimed throughout the
world, what she has done will be told in remembrance of her" (14.9).
Can our Lord commend us by our lavish actions to Him, especially in

126

serving others? To-day we should ponder hard on the implications of Mary's loving act to her Master.

Once resolved to come to Jerusalem, Jesus is fearless. He knows only one thing, and that is to do His Father's business. And His business and that of the religious authorities in Jerusalem are not the same. Holy Monday has been linked traditionally with Our Lord's cleansing of the temple and doing so Jesus was directly challenging the hypocrisy of the Jewish religious leaders. The temple was built for God and for His people to come there to be with Him in prayer. "For thither the tribes go up, ... to give thanks unto the name of the Lord" (Ps.122. 4). However it had become "a den of thieves". In a sense Jesus threw down his gauntlet!

Just as Jesus challenged the hypocrisy of these religious leaders, so does He challenge and confront every kind of hypocrisy and insincerity, all cheating and deceitfulness in our lives and societies. Any act that cannot stand the piercing glare of Christ has to be purged from us. Hypocrisy is the direct opposite to purity, and thus we have to remember our Lord's saying that only "the pure in heart" will be able to see God, and enter His kingdom.

Put in the form of another of Our Lord's teaching, we cannot serve both God and mammon. In our quest for holiness all dross must be purified. We have to let the Spirit be like a shower of rain falling on hard frosty ground. Bit by bit the water soaks into the ground until the frost begins to melt.

As Christians we are called to cleanse our lives in the purity of Christ's teaching. This means we keep our bodies pure as they are the temples of the Holy Spirit. For the latter this means that we do not abuse our bodies sexually or through drugs or by over indulging in eating and drinking, or by being slovenly and lazy. The basis for any Christian relationship is honesty. I know some people say that if one is too honest, then that can hurt others and therefore it is more preferable to tell a white lie. The Pauline tradition tells us very clearly we must speak the truth in love and in Christ as he did (Eph. 4.15 & 1Tim. 2.7). Anything other than the truth is a deception, and any kind of deception immediately forms a barrier. From some of my own experiences when very painful things have had to be said, although the person with whom you are conversing has been upset, most visibly at times, I've always known that person in the end to acknowledge truth is kinder than any hedging. The other side of all this is that the person having to speak the truth experiences pain too because she/he knows the immediate suffering of the other. The most important thing is to remember that God is in that situation, and if we are sensitive enough to Him, He will be the Speaker. Another factor to be considered is that quite often people are more resilient than for what we give them credit. Sometimes too people have some kind of premonition of the truth. This is especially true in regards to breaking the news of the death of a loved one.

We are also called to live honest lives where we work: in offices, behind check-outs or computers, retail business etc. That means working to the best of our ability and using our work hours for the employer and not for our own. There seems to be the temptation to think that the most important criterion is to sign on each day, and how we spend that day is not of any great consequence. Or there is the attitude that the company's resources are there for our use too, and therefore there is nothing wrong about helping ourselves to stationery, pens, clips and so on. In a sense this would be a bit like picking up the clean cutlery left on a host's table after having been invited to dinner and going home with it. I don't think anyone would do this, and would be deeply insulted at the suggestion of such a thing, but why the two standards?

Holy Monday therefore demands us to examine our lives to see whether they glow with Christ's purity and honesty, and to examine whether we live by Christ's commandments or our own watered down version of them. After confronting ourselves through Christ's eyes, the comforting factor of this day is that we can be cleansed of all that is not pure and honest within us.

On this Holy Monday let me dig deep to discover the impurities within me dear Lord through the cleansing power of Your Spirit. By acknowledging them let my actions and thoughts from now onwards be such that they can withstand Your penetrating Light. Amen.

HOLY TUESDAY

AUTHORITY

Now is the Son of Man glorified.

John 13.31.

Full Readings: Isaiah 49. 1-6; Psalm 7.1-6, 15-7; John 13. 21-33, 36-8.

OUR LORD SPOKE THE above words after stating that one of His disciples would betray Him, and it would be the one to whom He gave the morsel of bread. That person was he who then went out into the night. As to-morrow's Gospel reading is that passage from Matthew when Judas arranged such betrayal, I shall leave further discussion on the betrayal for the morrow.

To-day I shall concentrate on the traditional reflection for Holy Tuesday, the day of questions. As Jesus continued to teach in the temple He was approached by the chief priests and elders about His authority to teach. Rather than give a direct answer He counter questioned them about the baptism of John. They are trapped, which no doubt infuriated them even more, especially after listening to the parable of the wicked tenants. Then the Pharisees tried to ensnare Jesus through His disciples by asking them, "Is it lawful to pay taxes to the emperor or not?" Jesus aware of their malicious intent answered for them and for us too that we must pay our taxes (Mk 11.27–12.18). So on this day of questions Our Lord made it quite clear that His authority comes from God, but at the same time He recognized a princely authority in this world, and that His disciples and we live under that authority too. In others words Christians live in a political state, as well as the heavenly, and both require our obedience. Therefore as

129

Christians we have to respect the authority of the state in which we live, and if we object to any of its laws, it must be done through the right channels. Being a Christian does not give us the right to ignore laws of our country, but it does give us the right to challenge them and work towards their change or alteration if they are unchristian through the proper process.

By what authority did Christ challenge them? He challenged them by that higher authority which is His from His Father. His authority is able to penetrate the souls of all and so it unveils the narrowness, the rigidity and above all the hypocrisy of the Pharisees. In their ostentation of piety they had forgotten what humility and compassion were all about. In insisting on dotting every "i" of the law, they had forgotten the heart and purpose of it, and in their insistence of tithing on the least things they had forgotten the spirit of the law.

Our Lord thus broke more than convention and rules when He openly condemned how these religious authorities have misinterpreted the whole concept of the Law by insisting on outward observances but ignoring the spirit and mercy of it. Furthermore he advocated to those listening to His teaching not to follow the hypocrisy of their religious leaders.

This Holy Tuesday God's authority must confront us. We have to ask ourselves by whose authority do I live? It is not mine, certainly not the State's, but God's as the giver of all life. However sometimes we forget that God is the supreme authority, and allow ourselves to be captivated by seducing demonic powers such as drugs, alcohol, peer pressure and other satanic ways. If we allow this to happen for too long then we shall end up like the Pharisees having a hollow sound to our lives.

Even Christians who try to live under God's authority must allow that authority to penetrate their very being on Holy Tuesday to determine whether their life is pharisaic at all. It is all so easy to be seen praying in church, but are we really praying? It is all so easy to be caught up with the angelic singing of the choir and yet not to be thinking of God at all or why we are in a church or chapel. It is all so easy to set an hour aside for prayer and then spend most of it day dreaming. It is all so easy to visit someone in hospital and think this is my good deed for the day. And so one could go on! What it means that it is almost too easy for us to be like the Pharisees, "whited sepulchres, which indeed appear beautiful outward, but are within full of dead men's bones, and of all uncleanness" (Mt. 23.25). So what Christ said about the Pharisees He could also say about us.

If we take Holy Week seriously we must heed our Lord's warning that we must not be outwardly what we are not inwardly. If we learn to be humble and not seek any kind of exaltation then we shall not fall into the Pharisees' trap. Indeed we shall not be far the kingdom of God.

Heavenly Father, on this Holy Tuesday let me submit myself to Your authority in all that I do, knowing that if I submit completely I shall not live like the Pharisees by seeking recognition, but in humility silently rejoicing that I am able to do Your will. Amen.

HOLY WEDNESDAY

BETRAYAL

Judas Iscariot, went unto the chief priests,
And said unto them, 'What will you give
me, and I will deliver Him unto you?'
And they covenanted with him for
thirty pieces of silver.
And from that time he sought
opportunity to betray Him.

Matthew 26. 14-6.

Full Readings: Isaiah 50. 4-9; Psalm 69. 8-10. 21-2, 31-4; Matthew 26. 14-25.

WHAT MAKES A FRIEND betray a friend as friendship implies trust? The underlining reason is that we love ourselves more than our friend, which in fact means we use a person under the pretence of a friend for what for we can gain. Judas knew that Christ had incensed the religious authorities since His return to Jerusalem with His outspokenness in exposing their hypocrisies, and more than ever they wanted His arrest. The situation was such that Judas realized he could gain from it, irrespective of what consequences that might mean for Jesus. He thought simply of himself when he went along to the chief priests to see what he could gain from it all. What Judas did is what so many of us do. By merely concentrating on self, and not others, we never think through what are the consequences of our actions for us and for others. Perhaps if Judas had stopped for a moment to rethink the whole situation he may have seen that his betrayal would lead to

132

Christ's death. He then may have not gone to the chief priests. But man without grace is such an ego-centric being!

Judas' selfishness and greed are juxtaposed in the Gospel with the selflessness and loving devotion of Mary who, as custom was for the traveller on entering a house, washed Jesus' feet. But instead of water she used an expensive ointment and lavished it upon her Master's feet, and then dried them caringly and tenderly with her hair. She showed Judas and to the whole world what true friendship is, "to give and not to count the cost ... to labour and not to ask for any reward". John tells us that Judas quibbled over this lavish gesture of Mary, intimating that his love of money and his greed had become such heinous sins that they were eating into his soul. When these sins are not repented they become cancerous and if untreated will kill the soul as illustrated in Judas.

Andrewes in his 1593 Lenten sermon contrasted the difference between Mary and Judas.

> ...for she did not drop but pour; not a dram or two, but a whole pound; not reserving any, but breaking box and all; and that not now alone, but three several times, one after another.
>
> This she did; and, as it may seem, the coherence fell out not amiss. This outward ointment and sweet odour she bestowed on Christ for the oil of gladness, or the spiritual anointing (as St. John) and the comfortable savour of His knowledge (as St. Paul calls it), He bestowed on her.
>
> This, as it was well done, so was it well taken of Christ; and so should have been of all present but for Judas, says St. John. Who, liking better *odorem lucri ex re qualibet* than any scent in the apothecary's shop, seeing that spent on Christ's head that he wished should come into his own purse, repined at it.[104]

This Holy Wednesday we have before us two options: the selfless loving and caring of Mary towards her dear Lord, and the selfishness and greed of Judas who used Jesus for his own ends. Friendship as I said implies trust, and when we make a person a friend it means we love that person, despite what. From that moment we always try to think and anticipate their needs before ours; we desire the best for them. Yet how often have we been a Judas rather than a Mary and

---

104 Ibid., Vol. 2, p. 38.

let a friend down? How often have we simply used another person, hoping that we might gain something from it? Sometimes we might even do this unconsciously. We do have to keep examining our motives so that we are not exploiting another human being. Ideally in a Christian community, the corporate body of Christ to which all the baptized belong, we share and gladly share our gifts, talents and personalities with our brothers and sisters. In this kind of community the self is fused with the core so that in the sharing of life the self is always part of the whole; it can never be separated from it because the influences, beliefs and personalities of others are absorbed and mingled with our own. With such Christian sharing we forget what was originally ours, if ever that were the case!

Our Lord commended what Mary did, and He must have agonized over Judas' deed, especially in the light of His teaching to His disciples that "Greater love has no man than this, that a man lay down his life for his friends (Jn 15.13). Even after betraying our Lord, Judas committed a greater wrong in being unrepentant of his deed, and died in a state of hell, that is, without Love. He was not there to greet the Risen Lord on Easter morning but Mary was? Will we?

This Holy Wednesday we can also learn from the disciples' reaction to Jesus' remark during the Supper, "One of you will betray me." Instead of pointing the figure at one another, they soul searched, "Is it I, Lord?" We too can look inwardly in preparation for the Triduum, and perceive in what ways we betray our blessed Lord.

Dear Saviour, let me be like Mary and believe in You as my Friend as well as my Lord and Saviour. Help me not betray You by my actions and words, and especially not by selfish acts of greed and exploitation. Amen.

THE TRIDUUM

THE TERM "TRIDUUM" MEANS three days, and is applied to those three special days beginning on Holy Thursday. During this time the Church celebrates the events of the passion, death and resurrection of Christ in the most important liturgy of the whole year in three acts. The season of Lent concludes on Holy Thursday morning and that evening the Triduum begins with the washing of feet, the Last Supper, the stripping of the altar and the vigil before the Altar of Repose. Good Friday continues with the reading of the Passion narrative, the veneration of the cross and the receiving of the Sacrament from the tabernacle from yesterday's Mass. Holy Saturday witnesses the final act with the lighting of the new fire and paschal candle, the liturgy of the Word, the renewal of baptismal vows and the first Eucharist of Easter. All Catholics should be present for all the acts of this Liturgy.

HOLY THURSDAY

(Washing of the Feet, The Last Supper, and The Watch)

VIGILANCE

After Jesus has washed their feet, had taken his garments,
and was sat down again, he said unto them,
'Know you what I have done to you?'

John 13.12.

Full Readings: Exodus 12. 1-8, 11-14; Psalm 116; 1 Corinthians 11. 23-26;
John 13. 1-15.

IF WE TAKE SERIOUSLY being a Catholic this night ushers in the most
holy time of the Christian year. It is a privileged time for it gives
us the opportunity for the next three days to live completely with
Christ, as everything else fades into oblivion. The Church's liturgy
is so structured that we can all share in the events of our Christ's
life from Holy Thursday to Holy Saturday. To-night we are with Our
Lord as He washes the disciples' feet, has His last meal with them,
prays in the garden of Gethsemane before being arrested and put
on trial. The Gospels vary in detail about these events, but they all
acknowledge that Jesus suffered at the hands of Roman and Jewish
authorities. No wonder He has very little strength to carry the cross
outside the city for His crucifixion! We too will live out these events
through our vigil before the Altar of Repose this night.

At the Eucharist the Gloria is sung as it is a joyful occasion before
the gloom of Good Friday (and before it resounds even more glori-
ously at the Paschal Vigil Liturgy). It is indeed a joyful and glorious

136

occasion because on this night our Lord gives us Himself in many ways, almost too many. Firstly He gives us His example of humility in washing the disciples' feet, and His command to love one another. Secondly He gives us that means of always having Him in our midst through the Bread broken and the Chalice poured out until He comes again. This means we are never deserted by Him, even if we desert Him at times. The Sacrament means life and vitality and that is what we should take out in the world after each Mass. Nevertheless the joy of and thankfulness for the Sacrament make way for the other realities of this night: desertion and darkness. The church is stripped: now naked, devoid of life, there is nothingness. Jesus has gone to prepare for and meet His death.

Meanwhile the Sacrament has been taken to the Altar of Repose, usually in a chapel, which has been beautifully decorated to await Jesus. Here our dear Lord will rest for the night, and here He invites us to be with Him. If you have never experienced watching and praying with Our Lord on Maundy Thursday (the traditional name for this day taken from the opening word of the introit, *Mandatum*), I suggest you do it this year. Usually there is a roster system, mainly to ensure that there is always someone present, but one can come and go anytime. I can assure you it is the most wonderful night of the year. The silence envelopes you and penetrates deep within, so that you and Jesus become almost inseparable. You hear the silence of Jesus! This vigil is contemplation in all its sweetness. You want to linger and linger with your Lord, and you desire so ardently to be Mary so you could bathe those feet which will labour under the heavy cross and bear the nails. You simply pour out love, and time becomes almost timeless! A verse of a Eucharistic hymn will perhaps haunt you all night:

> Strength and protection may Thy Passion be;
> O blessed Jesus, hear and answer me;
> deep in Thy wounds, Lord, hide and shelter me;
> so shall I never, never part from Thee.[105]

Meanwhile for our Lord the hour has come! Judas has gone! Soon they will be here! Until then, the time is precious to be spent in unison with His Father so that the divine will may be done. As

---

105 *New English Hymnal*, p. 451.

the Paschal moon sheds it soft light over the garden of Gethsemane our Lord's soul is heavy. To support Him as He pours out His agony to the Father, he has taken Peter, James and John, the three who had shared with Him in His glorious transfiguration. His request to His friends is simple enough, to pray with Him. Yet they could not; they fail Him, their Friend and Master. Why? Was it because they were sleepy after the meal? Was it because they were lazy? Was it because they did not know for what to pray? For whatever reason they had deserted their Master and Peter was soon to deny Him as well. They could not watch with Jesus even for one hour!

As they slept Judas was gathering the troops. Only the moon silently watches as Jesus prays, and spreads her gentleness over His grief-stricken face. Soon the silence within the garden will be shattered by the sound of footsteps and the clamour of swords and staves, but more piercing will be the sound of Judas' kiss.

On this most holy night Judas' kiss challenges us to examine our loyalty to Christ; the disciples' sleep challenges the freshness of our prayer and meditation life, while the brutality of the soldiers challenge our absorbing the hurts of this life. It is too a time for deep-felt thankfulness for the Blessed Sacrament which is our Heavenly Food daily or weekly. Above all Jesus asks, on this most holy night, Will you come, and "taste and see how gracious is the Lord" and spend an hour or so with me? Will you?

Dearest Saviour, as I watch with You during the silent hours of this night let Your sufferings and grief penetrate deep within me so I can share something of what You endured for me and all mankind. Give me grace to love You above all else. Amen.

GOOD FRIDAY – THE CRUCIFIXION

GOD'S LOVE

It is finished: and He bowed His head,
and gave up the ghost.

John 19.30.

Full Readings: Isaiah 52: 13-52.12; Psalm 31; Hebrews 4. 14-6, 5. 7-9; John 18. 1 – 19. 42.

GOD'S LOVE WAS SUCH that it brought Him to Golgotha. It brought Him to dragging a heavy cross, often stumbling, often falling and needing support from a visitor to the city for the Passover festival. Outside the city where with two criminals He was nailed to His cross and left to hang until He died. What an ignominious death for the God of all creation, the Giver of all life and sustenance, to die bereft of any human dignity and little kindness. Such was God's love - a love that absorbed the cruelty of the cross - a cross which carried the sin of mankind.

> Sweetest wood and sweetest iron,
> Sweetest weight is hung on thee.

The cross is indeed sweetness for us, frail creatures, because in dying, Christ atoned for our fallen nature, and released us from the bondage of death. Like the Hebrews when they crossed the Red Sea, we are free from the tyrannies under which we live. We are washed clean in the water from His side, and in dying with Christ in our baptism we rise also with Him to a more glorious life. So Christ asks from the cross, "What could I do more for you that I have not done?"

Thus on Good Friday as we linger at the cross, our whole thoughts are directed to Christ there, hanging upon that cross. As we look and look upon our dear Saviour, we realize only too well the extent of God's love as well as our own sins of selfishness, anger, pride, hatred, jealousy, sloth, greed, impatience, intolerance and deceitfulness which drove those nails into His feet and hands, and made Him undergo such agony. O Lord never let You see my sins but through my tears. Never was there such a pitiful but merciful sight. Love outstretched to embrace all of mankind. "Come unto me," He says, "and I shall refresh you." Even in Your deepest agony, it was we You thought of!

Just as the sword pierces Your side, let it pierce our hearts to overflow and overflow with love for You, dear Saviour of the world. Just as the nails penetrated Your hands and feet, may they drive out all our sins. As You cried out "forgive them Father, for they know not what they do", we crave for your forgiveness for every time we have driven those nails in further. As You gave up Your Spirit, let us too die to sin every day. As we kneel and kiss a crucifix today during the Good Friday liturgy, may we do it lovingly and thankfully. May it enforce on us the weight of the Cross, and then see that weight in the glow of God's love. Perhaps those words of that wonderful Passiontide hymn written by Samuel Crossman during the Caroline Period, will ring in our ears as we do:

> *Here might I stay and sing.*
> *No story so divine;*
> *Never was love, dear King,*
> *Never was grief like Thine!*
> *This is my Friend,*
> *In whose sweet praise*
> *I all my days*
> *Could gladly spend.*[106]

Good Friday is a day of fasting and prayer, and at the end of it we should feel exhausted both physically and spiritually. With the vigil the evening before, we should have given so much that we are completely drained. It is only when we are drained, hungry, and fatigued that we can have any understanding of our Lord's passion. Don't be

---

106 Ibid., p. 133.

frightened to undertake all this for our Saviour. The savouring of it will last a long time. And if we do not spend Good Friday without any deprivation, how then can we taste the joys and wonders of Easter day, and enjoy that Queen of all festivals in celebration? We cannot!

So on this Good Friday spend and be spent for Him Who hang upon the Tree so that we may be His true sons and daughters. "What could I do more for you that I have not done?" That is the extent of God's love. Can we but love a little in response?

Dear Saviour, You have shown the extent of God's love for us, help me to respond to that love by loving You dearly in return. Amen.

Expectancy

Now in the place where He was crucified
there is a garden: and in the garden a
new sepulchre, wherein was never man yet
laid. There they laid Jesus.

John 19. 41-2.

THERE ARE NO EUCHARISTIC readings this morning as Holy Saturday is spent in the silence of the tomb. We await the first Eucharist of Easter in the evening.

The horror of yesterday has subsided. Jesus' body has been lovingly tendered for burial and placed in the sepulchre. There is a hush over the garden after the clamour of the crowds and the hammering of nails of yesterday.

Holy Saturday is a day spent in quiet expectancy waiting for "Judah's Lion [to] burst his chain". It is a very low-key day but a day of solemnity. It is therefore a day of preparation, and by now we should have made our confession for Easter. If there is any bitterness, grudge or anger we must relent and bear the spirit of forgiveness towards all. We must be ready to greet the Risen Lord. Nothing must hinder our reaching out to Him as Mary did in the garden.

Traditionally on Holy Saturday we ponder too on our Lord's preaching to all the departed. The Church has always taught that on this day Christ descended into Hades, the place of the departed spirits. One of the most moving accounts of our Lord in Hades, His conquering of evil and death, and raising the dead is given in the

Gospel of Nicodemus. So powerful is it, I would like an extract to be the focal point of our Holy Saturday's meditation.

> Satan, the prince and leader of death, says to Hades: 'Prepare yourself to receive Jesus who boasts that He is Son of God.'...
>
> Hades, answering, said to Satan, 'Who is this man so powerful, though He be a man who fears death? ... If therefore you are all powerful, of what kind is that man Jesus, who, fearing death resists your power?' ...
>
> And Satan answered, 'Why have you doubted and feared to receive that Jesus, your adversary and mine? ... His death is nigh at hand, that I may bring Him to you, subject to you and me.'...
>
> And while Satan and Hades said these things one to another, there came suddenly a voice as of thunders and a cry of spirits. 'Lift up your gates you princes; and be you lifted up, you everlasting gates, and the King of glory will come in.' ...
>
> And all the multitude of the saints hearing these things said to Hades .... 'Open your gates, that the King of Glory may come in.'
>
> And David said to Hades 'And now, O most vile and filthy Hades, open your gates that the King of Glory may come in.'
>
> And while David so spoke, the Lord of Majesty came upon Hades in the form of man, and lighted up the eternal darkness, and rent the indissoluble chains, and the aid of power invincible, visited us who were sitting in the deep darkness of trespass and in the shadow of the death of sins.
>
> Then Hades and Death and their wicked servants seeing this, together with their cruel ministers feared exceedingly the brightness of this great light revealed in their own realm as they saw Christ suddenly in their home, and they cried out, saying: 'We are conquered by You.' ....
>
> Then the King of Glory with His majesty trampled on Death, and seizing Satan ... delivered him to the power of Hades and drew Adam to His brightness. ...
>
> Then Hades [reviling Satan] said, 'Lo, now this Jesus, with the splendour of his divinity, disperses all the darkness of death and has broken the firm foundation of our prisons, and has sent forth the prisoners and loosed them who were bound; and all who were wont to groan under our torments, insult us, and by

their prayers our dominion is stormed and our kingdom conquered, and the human race no longer fears us.' ...

And the Lord, stretching forth His hand said, 'Come to me, all my saints who have my image and my likeness. You who by the tree and the devil and death had been condemned, see now how by the tree, the devil and death have been condemned. And immediately all the saints were gathered together under the hand of the Lord.' ...

And the Lord stretching forth His hand made the sign of the cross on Adam and on all His saints, and holding the right hand of Adam ascended from the lower world, and all the saints followed Him. ...

And all the saints [declared] 'Blessed is He who comes in the name of the Lord. The Lord is God, and has shone upon us. Amen. Alleluia.'[107]

Holy Saturday is also a day of reflection, to look back on the Lent we have just kept and to see whether it has been a time of growth for us. Has it brought us to live a life that pursues holiness more and more? That is, have we come to know God better and to love Him more deeply, and especially in the way we have lived towards our fellow brothers and sisters? Hopefully we can all say, I have grown, even if only a little. It is progress, progress towards perfection in Christ which is the goal and purpose for every Christian. Having made that progress, we have to remember that living the Christian life is not static. We have to build on our Lenten foundation during the whole year. If that foundation has been solid, we may stumble but we shall not sink under the various trials and temptations which await us from day to day, and we shall pray more. Amongst all the changes and chances of this fleeting world, we can repose upon God's changelessness.

On this Holy Saturday dear God, may I wait in quiet expectancy to meet You as the risen and triumphant Lord. Let me to do all that is needed to be ready for such an important and wonderful meeting so that sin and any kind of shadow will not dim that glorious Light. Amen.

---

107 Nicodemus, pp. 100-109.

TRIUMPH

> Rejoice, heavenly powers!
> Sing choirs of angels!
> Exult, all creatures around God's throne!
> Jesus Christ, our King, is risen!
> Sound the trumpet of salvation!
>
> The opening of the *Exsultet*.

Readings for the Mass: Romans 6. 3-11; Psalm 118.
Cycle A: Matthew 28. 1-10.
Cycle B: Mark 16.1-8.
Cycle C: Luke 24.1-12.

EVIL HAS BEEN OVERCOME! Death has lost its sting! Where now is the victory but through Christ Himself? As we huddle usually in the cold as well as the dark awaiting the lighting of the fire for the new light our thoughts should be towards that new life that we are about to celebrate, that life God gives us through the Second Person of the Trinity in His triumph over the grave. It is the most important celebration of the Christian year. As "the light of Christ" is chanted three times by the deacon as he carries the paschal candle into the church we are reminded too of how God separated light from darkness in the initial creation. Now as the new creation begins it is Christ's light only that will bring us out of darkness.

   To-night's liturgy has three parts: the proclamation of the Word; the initiation rites and the celebration of the first Eucharist of Easter. In the first part the readings declare God's saving acts to the Israelites as He delivered them from bondage in Egypt and set them on course to the Promised Land. Indeed the *Exsultet,* the Easter Proclamation, intertwines the two Passovers clearly – the Passover of the Israelites and that of Christ. Listen carefully to the words; they are indeed beautiful.

> This is our Passover feast,
> when Christ, the true lamb, is slain,
> whose blood consecrates the homes of all believers. ...

The second part is the initiation rite for catechumens and the renewal of baptismal vows by the congregation. For the catechumens it is the culmination of a long period of preparation to be become Christ's own. They "have been buried with Christ" in their baptisms, and have risen "with him to a new life." They are now inheritors of His kingdom.

The last part, the Eucharist, begins with the sound of bells and organ as the Gloria is sung. That heralds the joy of knowing that Christ is risen and that we shall receive that life at Communion. In due time, we pray that we too may be brought to the glory of the resurrection promised by this Easter Sacrament.

The Gospel reading tells of the women coming to the tomb very early in the morning with their spices after the ending of the Sabbath. To their surprise the stone had been rolled away and an angel appeared unto them exclaiming that Christ had risen and they must tell the disciples. Could this be true? After all it was not many hours before that Mary Magdalen and the other Mary had sat opposite the tomb. But then there had been the Sabbath observance! Nevertheless they set out, only to be greeted by the Master Himself. What joy they must have felt as they embraced His feet!

This night begins another year of living in the spirit of the risen Christ. Although there are fifty days to celebrate Easter in a very special way, we must remember that each Sunday the Eucharist is celebrated essentially to honour the Resurrection (that is why the transferring of other holy days to Sundays as the modern trend is, is not commendable).

We have finished Lent and the Triduum. Hopefully we are all more disciplined, prayerful and loving. It is so easy to say we can leave all that until next year. Of course next year may not come. This special time of the year has prepared us for how we should live each day. We do not know when that moment will come when we face our passover. Pray that we are not found wanting.

O heavenly Father we rejoice to-night with the angels and arch-angels in proclaiming the greatest news ever – that Christ is risen and had triumphed over death and sin. By Your grace help me to live like an Easter person. Amen.

EASTER DAY

CELEBRATION

The first day of the week comes Mary Magdalene early,
when it was yet dark, unto the sepulchre, and sees
the stone taken away from the sepulchre.

John 20. 1.

Full Readings: Acts 10. 34, 37-43; Psalm 128; Colossians 3. 1-4; John 20.
1-9.

IN MANY PLACES THROUGHOUT the world the Paschal Vigil Mass is
observed just before dawn on the Sunday. To me this is the more
meaningful experience as we enter the church in darkness and come
out in light and hopefully sunshine. When the morning is just about
to break we want to be like the holy women and run to the Easter
garden. There is something very moving and authentic to light the
first fire of Easter in the quiet sombre, just before the first streaks of
light intrude. Then at the appropriate time these first streaks give
way to the fullness of light as the sun fills the church and penetrates
our souls with its warmth and light as the Liturgy moves towards
the Eucharistic celebration. As we leave the Church after our first
Easter Communion we are bathed in light, glorious light which has
dispelled the dark when we arrived. The world harmonizes with
the spiritual, and shouts to us "The Lord has risen", and we reply,
"Christ is risen indeed, Alleluia," or in the words of Mary Magdalen,
"I have seen the Lord!"

With great expectancy we await for the bells to ring out and the
organ to explode before the *Gloria* at the first Mass of Easter. What

an uplifting experience: all the fasting, the self-denials, time spent in prayer, selfless acts for others are all woft to heaven in this thunderous outburst, and return blessed threefold as the joy and wonder of Easter echo throughout the beautifully decorated sanctuary. The experience of the singing of that first *Gloria*, often accompanied with hand rung bells and even the tooting of whistles are like the applause given at the end of a very moving opera or play.

> Christ is risen and the evil ones are cast down.
> Christ is risen, and the angels rejoice.
> Christ is risen, and life reigns in freedom.
> Christ is risen, and the tomb is emptied of the dead.[108]

This is indeed a most glorious day when we celebrate our Lord's triumph over death and darkness and His victory over the grave. "For having risen from the dead [He] is become the first fruits of those who have fallen asleep to Him." Death is no longer to be feared, but through Christ's resurrection it is the gateway to a more a glorious life. This day is the dawning of hope for every creature born.

> Christ is risen from the Dead!
> Death by death does He downtrod;
> And in those whom Death has slain
> He bestows Life again.[109]

Easter day is a day of joy and celebration. For those who keep Lent properly, it is an occasion for celebration because during Lent we have tried to live very frugally and more so during Holy Week. Thus it is a time to enjoy not only those things we have denied ourselves for six weeks, but to share our feast and happiness with others. Nevertheless before toasting Easter with that rather special bottle of wine we have kept for Easter, we should spare a thought and prayer for those who live under the shadows of all different kinds of adversities in their lives, and for whom the Resurrection has little meaning. It is a day when our hearts overflow in gratitude for what God has done for us. What could call for more celebration than the knowledge that we have been freed from the tyranny of the old self, and

---

108 *Orthodox Manual*, p. 78.
109 Ibid., p. 76.

restored to our former glory under the new? Such knowledge makes us want to exclaim as George Herbert did when he wrote his poem for Easter:

> Rise heart, thy Lord is risen. Sing His praise
> > Without delayes,
> Who takes thee by the hand, that thou likewise
> > With him mayst rise:
> That, as his death calcined thee to dust,
> His life may make thee gold, and much more, just.
>
> Awake, my lute, and struggle for thy part
> > With all thy art.
> The cross taught all wood to resound his name,
> > Who bore the same.
> His stretched sinews taught all strings, what key
> Is best to celebrate this most high day.
>
> Consort both heart and lute, and twist a song
> > Pleasant and long:
> Or, since all music is but three parts vied,
> > And multiplied,
> O let thy blessed Spirit bear a part,
> And make up our defects with his sweet art.[110]

May the joys and thanks for this day of life, love and liberty burst forth from my inner being dear Lord. It is indeed Your dancing day as we celebrate Your triumph over all darkness and death. You are risen indeed! Alleluia, Alleluia, Alleluia!

---

110 Dorman, p. 53

APPENDIX I

A LENTEN EXAMINATION OF CONSCIENCE

Create in me a clean heart O God
And renew a right spirit within in me.

LENT IS THAT SPECIAL time when we want to make our lives more Christ-centred. The way we do this is by examining our consciences and measuring our lives against that of Christ. The next step is a true repentance and acknowledgement of our sins and falling short of the glory of God as Paul reminds us in Romans.

What follows is an outline for such an examination.
+ In the name of the Father and of the Son and of the Holy Spirit.
Amen.
Lord, I confess my sin is great;
Great is my sin. Oh! gently treat
With thy quick flower, thy momentary bloom;
　　Whose life still pressing
　　Is one undressing,
A steady aiming at a tomb.[111]

LORD, bless to me this Lent. Let me fast most truly and profitably, by feeding in prayer on thy Spirit: reveal me to myself in the light of thy holiness. Suffer me never to think that I have knowledge enough to need no teaching, wisdom enough to need no correction, talents enough to need no grace, goodness enough to need no progress, hu-

---

111 George Herbert in Dorman, p. 41.

mility enough to need no repentance, devotion enough to need no quickening, strength sufficient without thy Spirit; lest, standing still, I fall back for evermore.

Show me the desires that should be disciplined, and sloths to be slain. Show me the omissions to be made up and habits to be mended. And behind these, weaken, humble and annihilate in me self-will, self-righteousness, self-satisfaction, self-sufficiency, self-assertion, vainglory.

May my whole effort be to return to You; O make it serious and sincere persevering and fruitful in result, by the help of thy Holy Spirit and to thy glory, my Lord and my God.[112]

LORD, you have taught, "Blessed are the poor in spirit, for theirs is the kingdom of heaven", forgive me Lord when I have been proud and arrogant and put myself before others, especially those weaker than myself.

LORD, you have taught, "Blessed are the meek, for they shall inherit the earth", forgive me Lord when I have returned a wrong with another wrong, and when I have been angry in my heart and even in words.

LORD, you have taught, "Blessed are those who weep, for they shall be comforted", forgive me Lord when I do not bear my sufferings with trust in You, and when I fail to be compassionate towards others, especially those suffering any kind of hardship.

LORD, you have taught, "Blessed are those who hunger and thirst after righteousness, for they shall be satisfied", forgive me Lord when I show little interest for the injustices and inequalities in our world, and have been more concerned about my own safety and comfort.

LORD, you have taught, "Blessed are the merciful for they shall obtain mercy", forgive me Lord when I show little mercy towards others, perhaps seeing the speck in their eyes but ignoring the beam in my eye, and when I judge unnecessarily.

LORD, you have taught, "Blessed are the pure in heart for they shall see God", forgive me Lord when I have spoiled the beauty of my senses with any kind of self-indulgence, and when I have done anything without pure motive.

LORD, you have taught, "Blessed are the peacemakers for they

---

112 Milner-White, p. 21.

shall be called the children of God", forgive me Lord when I have broken relationships with selfishness and quarrelling, and when I have not worked for harmony in home and neighbourhood.

LORD, you have taught, "Blessed are those who suffer persecution for the sake of justice, for theirs is the kingdom of heaven", forgive me Lord when I have neglected to pray for my fellow Christians who face hostility and persecution in many lands, and all who face persecution for their beliefs.

GIVE me a loving and trusting heart dear Lord to practise Your teaching in my daily living, and so proclaim to others the virtues of Your kingdom. Amen.

This Lent:

LET me leave behind all those worldly things such as the hours spent in front of the television, reading the newspaper and dallying around the supermarket. I pray to the Lord.

LET me leave behind all those times that I simply waste time, especially in day dreaming and pondering on the future. I pray to the Lord.

LET me leave behind all those little ornaments and mementoes I treasure. I pray to the Lord.

LET me leave behind all those frills to life I do not need. I pray to the Lord.

LET me leave behind all those grudges I carry. I pray to the Lord.

LET me leave behind all those bundles of worries I carry. I pray to the Lord.

O tree of Calvary, send your roots deep down into my heart. Gather together the soil of my heart, the sands of my fickleness, the mud of my desires. Bind them all together, O tree of Calvary, interlace them with thy strong roots, entwine them with the network of thy love.[113]

A reflection from St. Augustine's Confessions

Late have I love Thee, O Beauty so ancient and so new; late have I loved Thee!

And behold Thou was within me, and I myself on the outside;

---

113 Indian Christian prayer in C.P.B., p. 224.

and it was there that I sought Thee.
And into those lovely things, which Thou madest,
All unlovely did I rush.
Thou wast with me, but I was not with Thee.
Those things kept me far from Thee, things that would not exist,
unless they were in Thee.
Thou didst call, and shout, and shatter my deafness:
Thou didst sparkle, and shine, and dispel my blindness:
Thou didst sendest forth Thy fragrance and I did breathed deep-
ly, and now I sigh for Thee:
I tasted and now do hunger and thirst for Thee;
Thou didst touch me, and I have burned for Thy peace.[114]

It is only when we have a clean heart after confessing our sins that we can approach this very special season. Thereafter we can seek Our Lord, first in the wilderness, then on the road to Jerusalem and finally at Calvary.

Welcome dear feast of Lent. I give thanks for the opportunity to take stock of my life and to free myself of any bad habits I have, and to see myself as You see me gracious God. Fill me with Your grace to follow You all the way to Calvary, so that like the faithful women I can stand at the foot of the Cross and behold Your suffering and death – death that gives me that great gift of eternal and glorified life. Amen.

---

114 Augustine, (*Confessions*. X. 27), p. 19.

APPENDIX II

STATIONS OF THE CROSS

DURING PASSIONTIDE, ESPECIALLY ON Fridays, meditation on the Stations of the Cross is a helpful way to make our Lord's Passion more meaningful. It's a way when we can come face to face with Christ as He carries His cross to Golgotha. The *via Dolorosa* exposes us not only to Christ's sufferings but also to our sins. By prayerfully following the fourteen stations, it should bring us to our knees, deeply penitent for our sins and what those sins cost Christ. It should also make us very thankful and full of gratitude to our Saviour who embraced all mankind lovingly on the cross.

Stations can be done either individually or collectively in church by walking from one station to the next after each meditation or at home through a devotional book and use of our imagination to visualize each station.

I realize that meditation on the Stations of the Cross is a rather private experience - something between you and Your Saviour. The following meditation is from my own experience, and it is therefore very personal. I offer this in the prayer that the Cross will pierce you, and in doing this will help you to enter more fully into our Lord's Passion, and to become more aware of the cost of sin. It brought Him to Golgotha!

Prayer for Preparation

As I prepare to walk the *via Dolorosa*, cleanse me of any earthly attraction; purify my mind of all thoughts other than You; clear my vision of all sights except Your image; Let me give my all to You who gave Your all to me. May this meditation bring me to a deeper awareness of Your Passion, be an expression of love and an opportunity to grow in love for You, my blessed Lord and Saviour. Amen.

The First Station
Jesus is Condemned to Death

We adore You, O Christ, and we bless You.
Because by Your holy cross You have redeemed the world.

> *Faithful Cross! above all other,*
> *One and only noble tree!*
> *None in foliage, none in blossom.*
> *None in fruit thy peer may be;*
> *Sweetest wood and sweetest iron,*
> *Sweetest weight is hung on thee.[115]*

Pilate has washed his hands of You, dear Lord, and handed You over to the Jewish religious leaders. By his action He has condemned You to death. You are already half dead through the whippings that made furrowed-like stripes down Your back, and the wreath of thorns with which they have mocked You, have pierced your head. O what a pitiful sight they had made of You!

Yet I must not condemn the soldiers too much for their treatment of You; they were doing their job as it were. But I do know what I am doing, and I know that my sins of selfishness, such as ignoring You as my Lord in so many acts, words and thoughts add to that pitiful sight. I too make those thorns penetrate deeper into Your skull and tear at Your flesh.

Forgive me Lord for the many times I fail You; have mercy upon me, and grant me grace to be more faithful to You. Amen.

The Second Station
Jesus Takes up the Cross

We adore You, O Christ, and we bless You.
Because by Your holy cross You have redeemed the world.

---

115 Instead of *Pange lingua, Stabat Mater* can be used.

Sing, my tongue, the glorious battle,
Sing the ending of the fray,
O'er the Cross, the victor's trophy,
Sound the loud triumphant lay:
Tell how Christ, the world's Redeemer,
As a Victim won the day.

The form of Your death is by crucifixion. That means Your already battered body must stagger under the weight of the cross as well, for You are expected to carry it to Your place of execution. That place is some way off; outside the city, to what is called the place of the skull. It is a long haul, and it will get heavier and heavier, and harder and harder to bear. There will be no mercy from the soldiers as You fall under its weight, but only help from a stranger in helping You to carry this cross.

Your cross dear Saviour is made so heavy because it bears the sins of mankind. My sins, my most grievous sins are part of that weight, and every time I sin, it makes it a little more heavy. I should be helping You bear that cross when You are so weak, but instead through my sins of weakness and laziness I am causing You to carry it alone.

Forgive me Lord for the many times I fail You; have mercy upon me, and give me Your grace to be more faithful to You. Amen.

The Third Station
Jesus Falls for the First Time

We adore You, O Christ, and we bless You.
Because by Your holy cross You have redeemed the world.

Faithful Cross! above all other,
One and only nobly tree!
None in foliage, none in blossom,
None in fruit thy peer may be;
Sweetest wood and sweetest iron,
Sweetest weight is hung on thee.

You have now set out for Golgotha my dear Saviour. As You

make Your way out of the city, the way is crowded with people, most of them jeering at You. What must hurt so much is that a few days ago when you entered Jerusalem these same people welcomed you as their King with their shouts of "Hosannas". Their cries this morning of "crucify, crucify" still ring in Your ears. Nevertheless You must press on, but the weight of that cross becomes intolerable and You stumble and fall under it. You collapse in the dust, and now Your face is brown as well as crimson! O my dear Lord, brought so low by that cross!

Yes, Lord, You are prostrate in the dust; the cross has brought You to this. As You struggle to get up and bear what You must, I have to watch that struggling, knowing that it is made so much harder because of my sins, my sins of greed and indulgences.

Forgive me Lord for the many times I fail You; have mercy upon me, and grant me grace to be more faithful to You. Amen.

The Fourth Station
Jesus Meets His Mother

We adore You, O Christ, and we bless You.
Because by your holy cross You have redeemed the world.

God in pity saw man fallen,
Shamed and sunk in misery,
When he fell on death by tasting
Fruit of the forbidden tree:
Then another tree was chosen
Which the world from death should free.

There was one who did not jeer at You along the way; her heart went out to You, indeed her heart must have been breaking as her eyes focused on You: Your blessed Mother. You are both bound together in grief, agonized grief, for one another. That sword which old Simeon has prophesied would pierce her heart, has. It has so pierced her, that her heart bleeds just as Your body and head are bleeding from Your terrible wounds. If Mary's grief is so galling, what must Yours be as You in turn to look upon her? As her Son, she has loved

You with a love that only a mother knows; You know this, and so before You die You will take care of her by committing her into the hands of the beloved disciple.

Mary grieved for You; her heart went out to You, and as a Mother prays she could have taken Your place, so that her Son would not have to suffer. I too look on Your face dear Lord, but in it, I see it bearing my sins, my sins of unconcern and uncaring for my fellow man. Let me grieve for them and for all my sins with the same depth that Mary grieved for Your suffering.

Forgive me Lord for the many times I have failed You; have mercy upon me, and grant me grace to be more faithful to You. Amen.

The Fifth Station
Simon of Cyrene Helps Jesus to Carry His Cross

We adore You, O Christ, and we bless You.
Because by Your holy cross You have redeemed the world.

Faithful Cross! above all other,
One and only noble tree!
None in foliage, none in blossom,
None in fruit thy peer may be;
Sweetest wood and sweetest iron,
Sweetest weight is hung on thee.

Shortly after setting out carrying Your cross Lord, You fell under the weight of it. As the soldiers whipped You, You struggle to get up, but it is almost too much. A stranger to Jerusalem, a man known simply as Simon from Cyrene is forced by the soldiers to help You bear that cross. It would be lovely to think he helped You willingly and not grudgingly. Oh, if he had known Whose cross he carried, he would indeed have carried it lovingly!

Unlike Simon, I do know Who you are; there are never any excuses for me, when You ask me to carry Your cross in the world. How often do I carry it with a listlessness. If only I would stop and think, I would realize that the cross you ask me to take up daily gives me my salvation. Then I would do it full of love. Instead I make the cross heavier for You by my sins, my sins of neglect and omission. O Lord when will I really begin to love You?

Forgive me Lord for the many times I fail You; have mercy upon me, and grant me grace to be more faithful to You. Amen.

The Sixth Station

Veronica Wipes the Face of Jesus

We adore You, O Christ, and we bless You
Because by Your holy cross you have redeemed the world.

> *Therefore when the appointed fulness*
> *Of the holy time was come,*
> *He was sent who maketh all things*
> *Forth from God's eternal home:*
> *Thus He came to earth, incarnate,*
> *Offspring of a maiden's womb.*

There were many women who had followed You during Your ministry Lord. What must they have felt as they saw the Man Who had healed, forgiven, fed and taught them staggering now under the weight of His cross as a common criminal? Amongst those women was Veronica. She represents all those women along the *via Dolorosa* who are weeping for You dear Lord and want to offer You a little bit of loving care to make Your load easier. With her clean handkerchief in hand, she steps forward from the crowd to meet You. As her eyes meet Yours, she tenderly wipes Your blood-stricken face, now clogged with the grime from Your falling. Tradition tells us for her loving act her handkerchief bore the imprint of Your face. Yet the real imprint for Veronica would have been visual enough. She would never forget Your blood-stricken face, lined with suffering You were enduring for mankind. You were touched by such tenderness in the midst of so much cruelty.

Lord, unlike Veronica, I have never spared enough time it seems to look at Your face, and see how it is bruised and bloody. If I did I would be moved to tears when I beheld that blood-stained face, and compassion for You would overflow. It would also help me to see You in the down and outs of our society and indeed everyone I meet. Instead those cuts to Your face bleed more profusely because of my sins, my sins of lack of compassion and empathy for my fellow man. Let me be like Veronica and look steadfastly into You face so that You shame me into wiping Your bloody face.

Forgive me Lord for the many times I fail You; have mercy upon me, and grant me grace to be more faithful to You. Amen.

The Seventh Station
Jesus Falls the Second Time

We adore You, O Christ, and we bless You.
Because by your holy cross You have redeemed the world.

Faithful Cross! above all other,
One and only noble tree!
None in foliage, none in blossom,
None in fruit thy peer may be;
Sweetest wood and sweetest iron,
Sweetest weight is hung on thee.

Despite Veronica refreshing Your face with her clean, cool handkerchief, the cross becomes heavier and heavier for You Lord. You try to carry on, but it all becomes too much, and You collapse once again under its burden. Who can blame You? Who would have got this far after the night of battering and torture You endured? As You fall for the second time, what do You feel and think? Your head must be spinning, You mind must falter and Your body must be exhausted. You are absolutely frazzled! Yet You must get up and somehow press on towards Golgotha for worst agony.

Your falling under Your cross, and rising once again should be a comfort to me Lord because I am always falling through my sins, my sins of deceitfulness and impurities. However I remain longer in the dust and grime than You did, and sometimes I am not very anxious about getting up. Make my heart pure, but not quite yet, is so apt! Yet You rose from the dirt in order that You could carry Your cross to make me pure in my love for You. Help me to be "pure in heart" dear Saviour.

Forgive me Lord for the many times I fail You; have mercy upon me, and grant me grace to be more faithful to You. Amen.

Eighth Station
Jesus Comforts the Women of Jerusalem

We adore You, O Christ, and we bless You.
Because by Your holy cross You have redeemed the world.

> *Thirty years among us dwelling,*
> > *Now at length his hour fulfilled,*
> *Born for this, He meets His Passion,*
> > *For that this He freely willed,*
> *On the Cross the Lamb is lifted,*
> > *Where His life-blood shall be spilled.*

When You entered Jerusalem for the last time, You had wept over it dear Lord because it was a city of disunity within itself, which would lead to its destruction. Now on Your last journey out of Jerusalem You offer this warning to the women who were following You with great lament and bewailing. Veronica, representing all the women following You to Golgotha had given You a sign of their love. But now when You fall again to the ground, more exhausted than ever, their grief for You is overwhelming, and their wailing over You penetrates to the depth of Your soul. You have to respond; You must, even in Your intense suffering, reach out to them and give them some comfort. So You assure them that Your own suffering will soon be over, and bid them to save their tears for themselves when their city will have worse suffering. Then they will have plenty to weep over!

I should weep and wail as the women of Jerusalem did when they beheld Your mangled body because I know that it is my sins, my sins of anger and bad temperedness that caused Your body to be so battered and bruised. Yet how often do I weep, let alone shed hot, bitter tears over them? Not often enough! No wonder dear Lord, You say to me not once but many times, "Weep for Yourself." O Lord help me to weep profusely from a deep contrite heart for all my sins, and give me such a loathing for sin which keeps me from You.

Forgive me Lord for the many times I fail You; have mercy upon me, and grant me grace to be more faithful to You. Amen.

The Ninth Station
Jesus Falls the Third Time

We adore You, O Christ, and we bless You.
Because by your holy cross You have redeemed the world.

Faithful cross! above all other,
One and only noble tree!
None in foliage, none in blossom,
None in fruit thy peer may be;
Sweetest wood and sweetest iron,
Sweetest weight is hung on thee.

You are almost to the place of Your crucifixion Lord, but before You reach Golgotha those last hundred yards or so seem like a thousand. You try to make it, but alas, Your frail body gives way once more. You buckle yet again under the sheer heaviness of Your cross, despite it being the means of redemption for mankind. Once again You grovel in the dirt as the soldiers' whips lacerate Your already torn flesh. How much more can You endure dear Lord? The authorities want You dead, but they have almost killed You before You reach Golgotha. Somehow You stagger to Your feet to bear that cross a little further to Golgotha.

My dear Lord, your are brought so low once again, as You grovel on the ground under the weight of Your cross, because of my sins, my sins of pride and arrogance. You have taught me so often through the Gospel, that I must be lowly and humble, yet still Lord I have not learnt that only the last will be first. Teach me that humility is the essence of living the Christian faith, and it is the only way I can truly be Your sister.

Forgive me Lord for the many times I fail You; have mercy upon me, and grant me grace to be more faithful to You. Amen.

The Tenth Station
Jesus Is Stripped of His Garments

We adore You, O Christ, and we bless You.
Because by your holy cross You have redeemed the world.

Bend thy boughs, O Tree of Glory,
Thy too rigid sinews bend;
For awhile the ancient rigour
That thy birth bestowed, suspend,
And the King of heavenly beauty
On thy bosom gently tend.

Lord, You have at last reached Golgotha, the place for Your crucifixion. Now the last preparations have to be endured. If you had any dignity left after the many floggings You endured throughout the night and along the *via Dolorosa*, You are now stripped of that, as You stand naked to the world and especially to the crowd which has gathered to see You and the two thieves to be crucified alongside You, as a piece of sport. You will have to endure the jeering until You breathe Your last. What agony it must have been for Your Mother to see You stripped of Your garment, a garment no doubt made by her loving hands. Worse still You and she have to witness the soldiers casting lots for Your seamless garment! Yet You do not hold this against them because as You say from the cross, "they do not know what they do". Such is Your humiliation, You bear it all so patiently.

However unlike the soldiers, I do know what I do. I know that You are stripped of every shred of dignity at Golgotha because of my sins, my sins of impatience and quick temperedness. I have condemned You to such humiliation and yet I do not crave for Your pardon readily enough. Dear Lord just as You were stripped of Your garment, let me be stripped of every sin, and when I do sin to recognize the weight of it upon your naked and crushed body.

Forgive me Lord for the many times I fail You; have mercy upon me, and grant me grace to be more faithful to You. Amen.

The Eleventh Station
Jesus Is Nailed to the Cross

We adore You, O Christ, and we bless You.
Because by Your holy cross You have redeemed the world.

Faithful Cross! above all other,
  One and only noble tree!
None in foliage, none in blossom,
  None in fruit thy peer may be;
Sweetest wood and sweetest iron,
  Sweetest weight is hung on thee.

It is about 9.00 (noon if we follow John's Gospel) when Your battered body is stretched out on the cross and Your hands and feet have to be nailed to it. You offer Your arms and the soldiers tauntingly place them on the horizontal beam. The pain is excruciating as the blows drive those nails further and further into Your hands in order to make You secure. Then You have to endure a similar process for your feet to be nailed to the vertical beam. As you are lifted up, Your head is swimming, Your whole body is faint with its physical agony, and You feel horribly nauseated. On either side of You there are the thieves and so Lord You have to absorb their suffering screams as well. Above Your head, You carry the inscription, "The Kings of the Jews", which only angers the jeering crowd that hurl out further abuses at You. Yet in the crowd there are some who love You. Besides the Blessed Mother there is Mary Magdalen, and the beloved disciple. Seeing Your Mother on the way, You know there is one last thing You must do while You can, and that is to assure that she is looked after. So You commend her into the care of the beloved disciple. You also assure the penitent thief of forgiveness and ease his pain. As the day darkens, You know that all has been done. Your cross is Love exposed to the world. Thus for You dear Lord the cross is embraced and cherished. You beg all onlookers not to despise what seems to be a shameful death but to glorify in Your death as through it Love has conquered all the worst that this sinful world can do.

165

The soldiers were merely doing their duty when they hammered the nails into Your hands and feet, but I do it willingly by my sins, my sins of injustice and intolerance. Let those nails so pierce me to purge me of my sins. Help me to look up at the cross with the loving eyes of Your Blessed Mother, and then I shall see suffering as no man has ever endured. Such suffering You bore lovingly and freely for me and all mankind. Dear Lord help me never to deny You again, and cheerfully carry Your cross for the rest of my life.

Forgive me Lord for the many times I fail You; have mercy upon me, and grant me grace to be more faithful to You. Amen.

The Twelfth Station

Jesus Dies on the Cross

We adore You, O Christ, and we bless You.
Because by your holy cross You have redeemed the world.

> *Thou alone was counted worthy*
> > *This world's Ransom to sustain,*
> *That a shipwrecked race might ever*
> > *Thus a port of refuge gain,*
> *With the sacred blood anointed*
> > *From the Lamb for sinners slain.*

While the day takes on the appearance of night, the consummation of Your earthly life nears. You must die if man is to be renewed and restored to his former glory. The cross is thus exalted because on it Love dies for fallen humanity. It is Love lived as it should be, unconditionally. And yet before that consummation, Lord, You underwent grief, agony, loneliness, despair, torture, and pain. The worst of these must have been the loneliness and despair because there was no one to help. At that moment You and Your Father are one and so Your plea to the heavens goes unanswered. The only sounds You hear are the sniggering, the jesting and jeering of the crowd who yell out such abuses as "If You be the Son of God, come down from the cross", "He saved others; Himself He cannot save", and "He trusted in God; let Him deliver Him now, if He will have Him." Such shouting would not only have pained You, but it would also have made the heart of Your Mother and Mary Madgalen and the other faithful women ache even more. This You know, as You absorb their pains and the pains of all into that broken body. But now Lord all has been accomplished and You die on Your cross.

You die on the cross because of Your love for mankind. My sins, my sins of hypocrisies, unfaithfulness and carelessness have not helped. This is what sin has cost You, death in a most horrible and cruel way. Did it all have to be so bloody Lord? Could not it all have been more merciful? "No!" You answer, as sin is a messy business; it corrupts, it poisons, it devours! Only unconditional love can conquer. Help me now to leave all my sins there, nailed to Your cross, so that I can never again subject You to such suffering. Let me remember Your face, though blood-caked, full of love, Your outstretched arms welcoming me to You despite my sins, and Your shattered body offered so I may have eternal life.

Forgive me Lord for the many times I fail You; have mercy upon me, and grant me grace to be more faithful to You. Amen.

The Thirteeneth Station
Jesus Is Taken Down from the Cross

We adore You, O Christ and we bless You.
Because by your holy cross You have redeemed the world.

Faithful Cross! above all other,
One and only noble tree!
None in foliage, none in blossom,
None in fruit thy peer may be;
Sweetest wood and sweetest iron,
Sweetest weight is hung on thee.

It is finished dear Lord. Your suffering is all over. As You died so quickly, You were spared the additional agony of Your legs being broken. Instead they pierced Your side, just to make sure You were truly dead, but what flowed forth was life in the water of Baptism and Blood in the Eucharist. And so each day You continue to give us Your life in the Blessed Sacrament.

One of those witnessing Your death was a secret admirer - Joseph of Arimathæa who begged the authorities to have Your body. And so Your body is taken down from the cross to be prepared for burial. But before that Your Mother is there to cradle You for the last time, and to recall how often she did this when You were a child. Poor Mary, what agony it has been for her too. How often had her heart been pierced during these last twenty-four hours? That suffering she would take to her own death.

As my sins, my grievous sins, my most grievous sins caused Your death, may I suffer and endure some of that pain and agony you have undergone for me by dying on the cross. Every time I sin let me realize what that sin cost You. Help me to live so that Your death is not in vain. You came to free me from the tyranny of sin and self and to make me holy. O dear Lord I do not want to disappoint You ever again.

Forgive me Lord for the many times I fail You; have mercy upon me, and grant me grace to be more faithful to You. Amen.

The Fourteenth Station
Jesus Is Laid in the Tomb

We adore You, O Christ, and we bless You,
Because by Your holy cross You have redeemed the world.

He endured the nails, the spitting,
Vinegar and spear and reed;
From that holy body pierced
Blood and water forth proceed:
Earth and stars and sky and ocean
By that flood from stain are freed.

After the cruelties and indignities Your body had been exposed to, it is comforting to know that for Your burial, loving hands tender it. Nicodemus has joined Joseph of Arimathæa in the garden, while Mary and Mary Madgalen are also there. They anoint Your body lavishly with expensive ointments; all your wounds are cleansed and cared for, the rotten odour from torn and mangled flesh is replaced by sweetened and soothing perfumes. When all this had been lovingly done, Your body is wrapped in a clean and scented cloth for burial. Now, all that can be done for You is accomplished. Lord you are placed in a new sepulchre, and at last You are laid to rest. Rest and repose after the ceaseless clamouring of the last twenty-four hours!

Dear Lord help me to embalm that battered body of Yours with acts of devotion and to show my love to You in the way I live from now onwards. I have seen what sin has done to You, and I am truly sorry for all the pain and agony I have caused You. Above all You have shown me what love is; help me to live as love should.

Forgive me Lord for the many times I fail You; have mercy upon me, and grant me grace to be more faithful to You. Amen.

Closing Prayer

Thanks be to You O Lord for all the insults You have suffered for me, for all the pain and torture You have endured, for through them You have redeemed me and shown me the way to live above sin. Never was their grief like Your grief, never was their torment like Your torment, never was there loneliness like Your loneliness, never was there thirst like Your thirst for souls. You have done all this because You love me and everyone so much that You want us all to enjoy eternal life. Thank You dearest Lord, let my whole being praise You now and for ever. Amen.

Sweetest wood and sweetest iron,
Sweetest weight is hung on thee.

+ + + + + + + + + + + + + +

Printed in the USA
CPSIA information can be obtained
at www.ICGtesting.com
LVHW082255130224
771731LV00018B/22